REPAIRING THE DAMAGE

Earthquakes *and* Volcanoes

LINWOOD

REPAIRING THE DAMAGE
Earthquakes *and* Volcanoes

Dr Basil Booth

EVANS BROTHERS LIMITED

Evans Brothers Limited
2A Portman Mansions
Chiltern Street
London W1M 1LE

First published 1992
Reprinted 1996
First published in paperback 1997

Typeset by Fleetlines Typesetters, Southend-on-Sea
Printed in Spain by GRAFO, S.A. – Bilbao

ISBN 0 237 51797 3

British Library Cataloguing in Publication Data

Booth, Basil
     Earthquakes and volcanoes. – (Repairing the damage)
     1. Earthquakes – Juvenile literature 2. Volcanoes – Juvenile
     literature
     I. Title
     363.3'495

Acknowledgements

Editor: Su Swallow
Design: Neil Sayer
Production: Jenny Mulvanny

Maps: Jillian Luff of Bitmap Graphics
Illustrations: Andrew Calvert

The author and publishers would like to thank Edmund Booth
for his help in preparing additional material for Chapter Six.

For permission to reproduce copyright material the author and
publishers gratefully acknowledge the following:

Cover (top – earthquake damage in Alaska 1964) NOAA/EPIS,
GSF, (bottom – rootless lava flow from Kilauea volcano in
Hawaii) Hawaii Natural History Society, GSF
Title page (view across caldera of Tengger Volcano, East Java,
Indonesia) Gerald Cubitt, Bruce Coleman Limited **p4** (left,
right) Steve McCutcheon, Frank Lane Picture Agency **p5** S
Jonasson, Frank Lane Picture Agency, (inset) GSF **p6** (top)
Werner Layer, Bruce Coleman Limited, (bottom) Solarfilma,
GSF **p8** (top) S Silf, GSF, (bottom) Hawaii Natural History
Association, GSF **p9** Miessler/ECOSCENE **p10** (top) J D Griggs,
USGS, GSF, (bottom) GSF **p11** (left, right) GSF **p13** (top,
bottom) GSF **p14** University of Colorado, GSF **p15** Tony
Waltham, Robert Harding Picture Library **p16** (top) GSF,
(bottom) Winifried Wisniewski, Frank Lane Picture Agency **p17**
(left) Orion Press/NHPA, (right) Martin B Withers, Frank Lane
Picture Agency **p19** P Harris, GSF **p21** S Silf, GSF **p23** NOAA,
GSF, (inset) Steve McCutcheon, Frank Lane Picture Agency **p24**
(top) Steve McCutcheon, Frank Lane Picture Agency, (bottom)
University of California, GSF **p26** Mary Evans Picture Library
p27 Steve McCutcheon, Frank Lane Picture Agency **p28** Patrick
Fagot, NHPA, (inset) W Higgs, GSF **p29** (left) Patrick Fagot,
NHPA, (top right) Uwe Walz, Bruce Coleman Limited, (bottom
right) Robert Harding Picture Library **p30** GSF **p31** (main,
inset) GSF **p32** (left) Norman Tomalin, Bruce Coleman Limited,
(right) Hawaii Natural History Society, GSF **p33** S Jonasson,
Frank Lane Picture Agency **p35** GSF **p37** G Pinkhassov, Magnum
p38 Alex Webb, Magnum **p39** David Parker, Science Photo
Library **p41** (left, right) Ove Arup & Partners **p42** GSF **p43**
Michael Nichols, Magnum, (inset) Ove Arup & Partners

Some of the information on page 7 is taken from an article by Dr
Sturla Fridriksson, in Iceland Review 1984 Vol 4.
The eye-witness account on page 39 is taken from an article
'Looking back at Mexico' by Mr and Dr Adolfo Zeevaert, in Vol
21 No 5, May 1987, Earthquake Engineering Reasearch Institute
Newsletter. Some of the material in Chapter Six is based on
articles first published in issues of UNDRO (United Nations
Disaster Relief Co-ordinator) News. The illustration on page 34
was based on one in *Earthquakes*, published by HMSO, ©
Crown copyright 1983.

CONTENTS

INTRODUCTION

Every day an earthquake or volcanic eruption takes place somewhere in the world. Fortunately, many of these events are small, or take place in remote areas and are therefore of scientific interest only. Most earthquakes occur as tiny tremors that can be recorded only on very sensitive instruments. Volcanic eruptions take place constantly on the floor of deep oceans. It is only when life and property are threatened that we hear about 'new' eruptions and earthquakes through the media.

Man has been on Earth for less than one thousandth of our planet's life span. Yet despite the huge advances in technology our efforts are puny when compared with the immense forces of Nature. The 1783 eruption of Laki volcano in Iceland, for example, was 50 times more powerful than a one megaton hydrogen bomb and released 30 times more energy than the annual world production of electricity.

Throughout the world, major towns and cities have been destroyed by natural disasters which man can do little or nothing to prevent.

In China, earthquakes killed over three quarters of a million people in 1556, and half a million in 1976. One hundred thousand are believed to have died during the 1669 eruption of Mount Etna in Sicily, and the eruption of Krakatoa in Indonesia claimed the lives of over 36,000 people in 1883.

Large-scale disasters such as these take place every century or so. Smaller ones inflict death and suffering more frequently and although the number killed and injured are fewer, they remain an ever constant threat with which many people must learn to live. Repairing the damage after a natural disaster, without trying to minimise its effect before it occurs, is like closing the stable door after the horse has bolted. What we can do is minimise the effect of these damaging events by precise forecasting.

A winter street scene in Anchorage, Alaska, USA (below left) has changed dramatically by the spring (below), following the 1964 earthquake.

In 1973 a town on the island of Heimaey, Iceland (above) was buried under lava and ash (inset) when Eldjfell volcano erupted.

As we examine our planet's structure, we discover what causes the continents upon which we live to drift slowly about the face of the Earth, how this movement causes earthquakes and volcanism; how the seemingly solid rock on which we stand can snap to produce an earthquake in one place and flow like pitch in another. Armed with this information we can begin to understand how earthquakes produce giant killer waves and how volcanoes can wipe out huge areas within seconds.

Knowledge of how volcanoes and earthquakes behave makes it possible to calculate when and where an earthquake or volcanic eruption may take place. Maps can be produced to show where different kinds of hazards could occur, which local authorities can use to make emergency evacuation plans.

Strict control of building regulations in earthquake-prone areas may help save property and reduce the number of deaths, but only total evacuation of people from a potential disaster area saves lives on a really large scale. In terms of human suffering it is the Third World developing countries, which cannot afford costly forecasting schemes, that are most at risk. While the work of disaster relief organisations, such as UNDRO (United Nations Disaster Relief Organisation) and OXFAM go a long way towards alleviating the suffering, it will only be by the concerted efforts of scientists and closer cooperation between governments on a global scale that the impact of natural disasters on society will be eventually reduced.

CHAPTER ONE

ANATOMY OF VOLCANOES

Fireworks at sea

In Indonesia, between the islands of Java and Sumatra, there once lay a small island with three volcanic peaks. The central peak was called Krakatoa. It was here that the greatest volcanic eruption ever experienced by mankind took place. On May 20, 1883, Krakatoa volcano burst suddenly into activity, sending a plume of steam and volcanic ash nearly 10km into the atmosphere. Over the next few days the activity gradually increased, with fantastic lightning displays in the eruption cloud. A week later the eruption appeared to subside and surveyors were able to visit the island. They decided that although Krakatoa was still erupting, people living on nearby islands were not in any danger.

Then in August, the eruption suddenly increased in violence, hurling out pumice and ash clouds which rose to 27km, with strong explosions every few minutes. Towards the end of the month the eruption entered its final and most disastrous phase, with explosions that could be heard 1100km away.

At the time, the captain of a cargo ship was sailing through the Sunda Straight, a narrow channel of sea between Java and Sumatra. He wrote in the ship's log:

'The deafening explosions sounded like heavy gunfire while lumps of gas-charged lava exploded in the sky, like gigantic firework displays. Just after 5pm the ship decks were bombarded with lumps of hot pumice; some as large as pumpkins! Ash fell so rapidly on the deck (15cm in 10 minutes) that crew members worked continuously to keep the decks clear.'

The captain used the glow from the erupting volcano as a beacon to navigate his ship through the Straight.

'Static electricity filled the air, causing spectacular lightning displays. Bright blue discharges constantly took place on the ship masts and rigging. This alarmed the crew, who feared the glowing discharges would fall off the rigging and set fire to the ship.'

On August 27, the eruption reached its climax. Volcanic ash rose as high as 80km, and probably drifted round the world three times. Near the volcano the sun was blotted out by the ash cloud for two and a half days. Explosions occurred in a continuous roar, but just after 10am came the largest explosion known on Earth. It caused pain in people's ears 50km away, and was heard across the Indian Ocean.

The detonations were caused when massive flows of red-hot volcanic ash entered the sea. The red-hot rock fragments cooled instantly when they touched water, converting their heat energy into steam explosions. The explosions created huge waves (called tsunami) up to 39m high, which flooded the low-lying coasts of Java and Sumatra. Whole villages were swept away by these killer waves, some of which travelled inland for up to 16km. In all, more than 36,000 people died as a result of these tsunami, either by drowning or from diseases that followed the destruction of water drainage systems.

After the eruption, a survey found that Krakatoa had completely vanished. For many years it was thought that the island had been blown to pieces by the explosions. But if Krakatoa island had really been blown to pieces, then large fragments of the island should have been found along the coasts of the Sunda Straight. Recent research has shown that such fragments do not exist. We now know that the island sank back into its own magma chamber, as the contents of the chamber spilled out into the atmosphere. Since 1883, renewed activity from the magma chamber has built up a new volcanic island.

Nature takes over

When Krakatoa erupted, the plants and animals on the island were killed by the ash and pumice that were hurled out of the volcano. But within a decade, plants and animals had re-established themselves on the island to such an extent that it was difficult to see the effects of the eruption. Access to the island was not limited, so it was difficult to know how many species had been brought in by visitors, and how many had arrived on the water and air. Eighty years later, scientists had an opportunity to monitor Nature more closely.

In 1963 a volcanic eruption on the sea bed off the coast of Iceland gave birth to an island now called Surtsey. The lava flowed for 18 months, and the island grew to an area of 2.5sq km. Access to the new island was strictly controlled and scientists have observed the spread of life on the island, from the first seeds to be washed up on the shore to the birds that now nest there.

The first plants to colonise the bare volcanic rock included sea rocket, lyme grass, lungwort and sandwort. Today, more than 20 plant species have been found on the island. Most of the seeds were carried to

Sea rocket, one of the first plants to grow on Surtsey

Surtsey by ocean currents. Gulls and geese, and migrating birds such as snow buntings have carried seeds on their feet and in their bodies.

Driftwood and clumps of grassy turf from cliffs on nearby islands drifted on the water, together with their cargo of seeds and tiny creatures. Cotton grass seeds have blown in on the wind, and spiders glided there on fine threads. Lichens and mosses colonised the lava and soil began to form from their remains. Black-backed gulls, fulmar and kittiwakes have already nested on the island, and others will join them as the vegetation builds up. Given time, Nature is able to heal most scars on the landscape.

Sea water pours into a vent of the Surtsey volcano and forms huge clouds of steam.

What is a volcano?

Every day, at least one volcano erupts somewhere in the world. Since many of these daily volcanic events are small and take place on ocean floors or in remote areas, they pass unnoticed. Volcanoes are really 'safety valves' that allow the pressure of pent-up gases to escape from the Earth's interior.

Most people think of a volcano as a cone-shaped mountain that spurts out fire, smoke and lava. This is only partly true. Some eruptions take place from a group of vents, while others take place from long cracks, known as fissures. These fissures can release immense volumes of lava, which destroys vast areas of countryside.

In 1783 an eruption from a fissure in Iceland released enough lava to cover more than 560 sq km of farmland. The lava destroyed crops, while the poisonous gases killed animals on the land, as well as fish in the sea surrounding Iceland. In the famine that followed, one fifth of Iceland's population died. The eruption also created a mini ice age in Europe as huge clouds of dust shut out the sun and prevented the snows of the previous winter from melting.

Not all volcanoes spurt out fire. Many do, but there are countless others that quietly release clouds of steam, gas (called fume), and 'smoke'. The 'smoke' is actually made up of cinder, fine rock dust and even blocks of rock. Rock material is worn away from the wall of the vent

Ngauruhoe volcano in New Zealand, releasing fume

Lava pours from a fissure in Hawaii.

and blown out by explosions deep below ground. In the lull between explosions some of this loose material falls back into the volcano crater, to be thrown out again in the next outburst of gas and steam.

Not far from Rome in Italy, there are two round lakes – Bolsena and Laziale – which hide potential killers. They are volcanoes that slumber peacefully for periods of 10,000 to 20,000 years between eruptions. When they do finally erupt, the effects are devastating. Rome, for example, is built on the deposits from several past eruptions from these volcanoes and if just one of them were to erupt again it could wipe out the entire city overnight.

In the past it was common practice to classify volcanoes as being either active, dormant or extinct, yet once every 10 or 20 years a so-called extinct volcano comes to life. This happened in New Guinea, when Mt Lamington erupted in 1951, sending clouds of red-hot gas and rock dust searing through its wooded slopes and killing 3000 people.

A volcano was counted as active if it had erupted during historic times (that is, the time since the eruptions were first recorded), or was actually releasing volcanic gases. Historic time, however, varies considerably throughout the world. For Mt Lamington it totalled 37 years, while for Mt Etna in Sicily, historic times began in 1500 BC.

It was because of this problem that the 1979 UNESCO conference produced a completely new classification scheme for volcanoes. Volcanoes that could erupt in the future are now called live, while those that cannot are called dead. When a live volcano is actually erupting it is active, and when it is not it is dormant.

Mt Etna, in Sicily, Italy, is a live volcano.

Volcanic eruptions

There are several types of volcanic eruptions. The three main ones are hawaiian, strombolian and plinian. Hawaiian type eruptions are produced from basalt magma. (Basalt is a volcanic rock rich in iron and magnesium.) Basalt magma is thin and runny, and allows volcanic gases to escape easily without explosive violence. The gases escape from the vent in a constant stream, hurling molten rock high into the air in spectacular fire fountains. If this molten rock falls while it is still fluid it flows over the ground in long streams. These are called rootless lava flows because they are not directly connected with the underground magma body. If the molten rock hardens in the air before it lands, then it may form 'bombs' of different shapes which hit the ground with force.

Since most of the gas is released at the main vent, the magma loses its gas content and flows quietly from openings (called boccas) lower down the side of the volcano. These lavas are thin and runny, which makes them dangerous. They flow like rivers for many miles, burning and burying all in their path.

Strombolian type eruptions are produced from lavas that are less runny than hawaiian ones. Because the lava is less runny it does not allow the volcanic gases to escape so readily and the eruptions are therefore more violent.

Strombolian eruptions produce spectacular fire fountains of mostly yellow-hot fragments of ash, cinder and bombs but rootless lava flows do not form. Large explosions in the vent tear rock from its sides and hurl it out as large blocks. These materials fall around the vent and build up a cone-shaped hill.

Some strombolian eruptions are small, taking place on the slopes of large volcanoes and forming very low cones. Other events occur in what are called 'live volcanic fields'. Such volcanic fields occur around Auckland in New Zealand, and in central Mexico. Volcanoes in these areas erupt only once and then die, and are called monogenetic volcanoes. It is the field that is live and it is the field that may produce many such eruptions during its life.

Plinian type eruptions are some of the most violent known. They are named after Pliny, a

Fire fountains and lava are produced during a hawaiian type eruption from a vent in Hawaii.

Roman who described the eruption of Mt Vesuvius in Italy in AD 79 (see page 14). In plinian type eruptions the magma is thick and pasty. This makes it difficult for volcanic gases to escape, so they build up to dangerously high pressures. When the pressure of these pent-up

A breadcrust bomb of pumice, named after its appearance.

A live (but dormant) volcanic field in Tenerife

A strombolian type eruption from Mt Etna, Sicily

gases is more than the pressure of the overlying rock, they blast the rock out with explosive force. Once released, the gases expand violently to produce a high eruption column, sometimes more than 48km high. The violence of the explosion shatters the gas-rich magma into small fragments, which are blown out in the eruption column. As these fragments reach the atmosphere the gas inside them expands and produces frothy white pumice. The eruption column reaches such heights that its debris falls like a snowstorm over wide areas, thickly mantling the nearby countryside with a blanket of white pumice.

Towards the end of a plinian eruption the gas pressure begins to fall. There is no longer sufficient gas pressure to pump ash high into the atmosphere and what is left is released to produce the most terrifying kind of volcanic eruptions known. One of two things may happen: the hot gas and pumice may pour out of the vent as a red-hot cloud, or the eruption may suddenly stop, leaving the eruption column unsupported. The column then collapses, the

Three main types of volcanic eruption

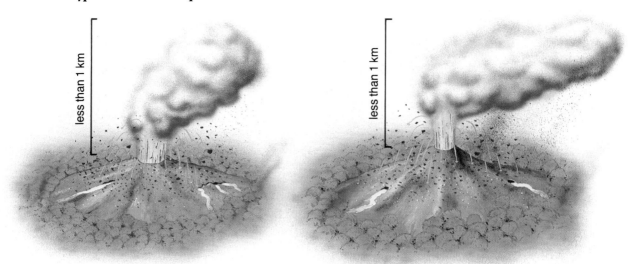

Hawaiian type

Some of the lava shoots up from the main vent in fire fountains, while some is released from boccas in the gently sloping side of the volcano. The thin, runny lava may flow for miles. The eruptive column is very low, and most of the ash falls close to the volcano.

Strombolian type

Strombolian type eruptions are more violent than hawaiian ones and the heavy rock material that is thrown out builds cones with steeper sides. The ash in the eruptive column may be blown several kilometres away from the volcano.

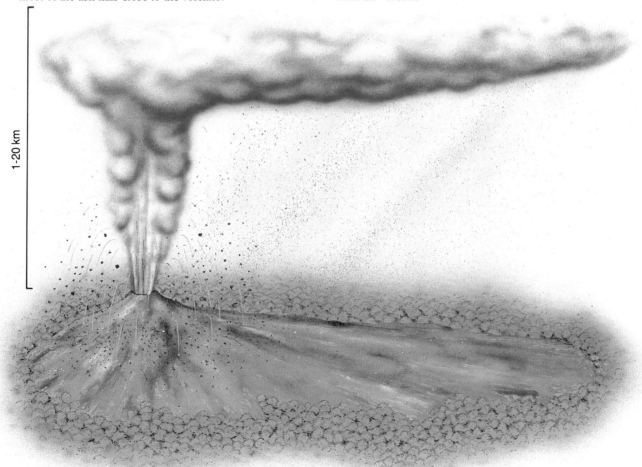

Plinian type

These eruptions are very violent and produce an eruptive column more than 20km high. The fine material in the cloud may fall to the ground up to 1000km away from the eruption. There are no lava flows, but sometimes the eruptive column collapses to form a nuée ardente, a red-hot cloud of ash and gas that rushes over the land and destroys all in its path.

red-hot clouds of ash and pumice fall to the ground and rush across the countryside at hurricane-like speeds as glowing avalanches, burning and burying all in their path. The Valles Caldera, USA, is a live volcano which has produced eruptions like this which have covered an area half the size of the state of California. North Island, New Zealand, has been the site of even larger eruptions of this kind and volcanoes have been discovered that have produced eruptions ten times larger than that of the Valles Caldera.

Only thin deposits are left by these immense eruptions. The massive blast has simply spread the large volume of ash thinly over vast areas. It is only the smaller events, which cannot disperse their products so widely, that build cones.

Amazing magma

Magma has four physical properties which in theory should not exist together. It is elastic, plastic, ductile and brittle.

Earthquake waves pass through magma because it is elastic. Magma can flow below and above the ground because it is plastic. It can be stretched to form the fine threads of Pele's hair (a volcanic rock resembling hair) because it is ductile, and during volcanic explosions it shatters into fragments because it is brittle.

The eruptive violence of volcanoes is controlled by the chemistry of the magma and is principally due to the amount of silica and aluminium it contains. In basic magmas such as basalt, these elements are completely used up to form minerals with small molecules and this produces runny magma. In acidic magmas, silica is not completely used up. There is sufficient silica and aluminium to form minerals with large complex molecules, and this produces thick pasty magma.

When the magma is thick and pasty the volcanic gases cannot readily escape. They accumulate and build up to dangerously high pressures, until released by a volcanic eruption.

Volcanic rocks

There are two basic kinds of volcanic rock. They are pyroclastic and non-pyroclastic. The term pyroclastic comes from the Greek, *pyro* meaning fire and *clastic* meaning broken.

Non-pyroclastic rocks are mostly lavas and there are three main types. Two have Hawaiian names: *aa* lavas have a rough clinkery surface with a solid interior, while *pahoehoe* lavas have a smooth, ropy and twisted surface, with a solid interior. Both are produced by eruptions on land. The third non-pyroclastic rock is called pillow lava. Pillow lavas are produced by underwater eruptions. In spite of their name, they are more like branching spaghetti than

Aa lava advancing over snow and forming small mudflows

Pahoehoe lava forms rope-like patterns as it cools and hardens.

pillows. Only when the ends of these complex branches break off do they resemble pillows.

Pyroclastic rocks are of two types. The first is produced during fountaining, when rock fragments are blown into the atmosphere and settle around and downwind of the vent to form air-fall deposits. The second is produced by glowing avalanches, known as nuées ardentes. When these clouds of red-hot dust come to rest and cool they form ash-flow deposits and ignimbrites. Ignimbrites are ash-flow deposits that are so hot when they settle that they weld together to form solid rock.

Cones and craters

Many big volcanoes have large, almost circular, craters on their summits, called calderas. These form during large plinian eruptions. The magma chamber below a volcano is emptied rapidly, leaving the upper part of the cone without a firm foundation. As the eruption progresses the top of the volcano slowly sinks into its own magma chamber. The volcano Krakatoa disappeared in this way in 1883 (see page 6). Calderas vary considerably in size from a few kilometres to tens of kilometres across. The Valles Caldera in New Mexico, for example, is 23km in diameter and that of the Long Valley of California measures 16km by 30km.

Preserved in pumice

The first accurate record of a volcanic eruption was made by Pliny the Younger in AD 79 in two letters to a friend. Pliny describes the eruption of Mt Vesuvius, in southwest Italy, and the death of his uncle, Pliny the Elder (a Roman writer).

In August AD 79 Vesuvius – the volcano that everyone believed to be extinct – erupted violently. Many people fled from the area. Within a few hours Pompeii and Stabiae were buried beneath as much as four metres of white pumice. When the eruption began, Pliny was staying at Misenum with his mother and his uncle. Misenum was situated at the north end of the bay of Naples, about 30km away from the volcano, and well out of harm's way. In the letter to his friend Pliny writes:

An eruption cloud collapses to form a nuée ardente.

'During the early part of the afternoon of August 24, my mother drew my uncle's attention to a large black cloud. It was unclear at the time from which mountain the cloud was rising, but it had the appearance of an umbrella pine, rising on a great trunk with branches splitting off. I thought it was due to the first blast, but it appeared to be left without support, for as the pressure subsided it sank under its own weight, spread out and dispersed. Parts of the cloud were white (steam) and parts were dirty due to the soil and ash it contained . . . My uncle called for a boat to be made ready [to get nearer to Vesuvius].

As uncle was about to leave he was handed a letter from Rectina, whose house was near the foot of Vesuvius. She was distraught and implored him to rescue her.

Upon learning this, my uncle abandoned his scientific trip for a mission of mercy and ordered warships to be launched at once.

Everyone was leaving the danger zone into which he bravely sailed. He ordered a scribe to note every phase of the eruption as he described it. As the ships approached the shore off Pompeii hot ashes were falling thickly, followed by pumice fragments and charred stones. The shore was so thickly choked with debris as they approached that they diverted to Stabiae, where he met his friend Pomponianus . . . .

. . . By now earth tremors were shaking the building, and the courtyard in which they stood was filling rapidly with ash. Tying pillows to their heads as protection against falling debris they set out for the shore to investigate the possibility of escape by sea, but they found it too rough and dangerous. A sheet was laid out on the ground for my uncle to rest, and he constantly asked for water to drink. Soon, the smell of sulphur warned of approaching fire. He was roused and stood up. For a moment he stood leaning on two slaves, then suddenly collapsed, presumably because the dense fumes blocked his windpipe.'

At this point Pliny's letter gives no more details on the events at the shore and it must be assumed that his uncle was left for dead. Pliny the Younger concludes:

'Two days later my uncle's body was found, uninjured and fully clothed, looking more like an old man asleep than one in death.'

It was because of Pliny's accurate description of this event that all volcanic events of this type are now called plinian type eruptions. Such eruptions are characterised by a continuous or steadily reverberating gas blast lasting from a few hours to two or three days, during which enormous volumes of volcanic rock are violently ejected in a rapidy rising eruption column. This ash and debris eventually falls like a gigantic snowstorm.

The ancient city of Pompeii has been well preserved under its layer of pumice. Excavation began in 1748, and work is still going on at the site to this day.

The ruins of Pompeii, with Vesuvius volcano in the background. The city was abandoned after the eruption in AD 79, and lay undisturbed for more than 1600 years.

CHAPTER TWO

SIGNS OF VOLCANISM

Fumaroles

Gases and water vapour escape from inside the Earth not only during volcanic eruptions, but through openings in the ground near volcanoes. The openings are called fumaroles. The hot gases emitted by fumaroles give volcanologists valuable information on the proportions of different gases in magma. By monitoring any changes in the fumarole gases, volcanologists forecast impending eruptions from nearby volcanoes. However, some magmas are so highly explosive that it is too dangerous for scientists

Sulphur crystals (inset) form round fumaroles (below).

to carry out tests on the gases they contain. Our knowledge of gases in such magmas comes mainly from laboratory work. In one experiment, powdered volcanic rock is put into a tiny capsule of pure gold, with a little water. The capsule is then sealed inside a glass tube. The capsule is heated electrically to a temperature of 2000°C. The water turns to steam, which cannot escape so great pressure builds up. Then the capsule is plunged into cold water. The rock powder forms a kind of glass. Scientists can cut thin sections of the glass to study the effects of heat and pressure on volcanic rock.

Fumarole gases contain water, carbon dioxide, acids and the salts of numerous elements. When the gases are released into the atmosphere, they condense and the salts are deposited around the fumarole vents. Yellow needles of sulphur and white crystals of chloride are among the most common incrustations. Other salts include green-coloured copper and nickel salts, pink-blue cobalt and lead, and pinkish manganese and zinc.

Hot springs and geysers

When there is a high proportion of water to gas, fumaroles become hot springs. The water slowly heats up as it circulates over hot rocks. As water heats up it expands, becomes less dense and begins to rise towards the surface. As it expands the gases dissolved in it are released as bubbles, which causes further expansion of the water, forcing it out through openings at the surface to form hot springs. Where the gas content is high the hot springs bubble vigorously, or eject fountains of steam and water called geysers.

Some of the world's best hot springs and geysers are found in Yellowstone Park in the USA, and Rotorua in New Zealand. In Yellowstone Park there are up to 10,000 active springs,

Japanese macaques keep warm by bathing in hot springs in Japan.

A hot spring beside a lake in Kenya

depending on the size of the vents counted. The waters that feed some of the springs rise through thick beds of limestone, dissolving it as they do so, and depositing it as travertine (a porous limestone rock used for building) around the openings.

The hot water cycle

Water in the ground in volcanic areas may be heated as high as 150°C and become superheated water. This temperature is well above the boiling point of water, but the superheated water does not boil because of its depth and because of the weight of water lying above it in the geyser pipe. Instead the water expands in the geyser plumbing system and forces the water above to overflow from the geyser vent at the surface. This reduces the weight of water lying on the superheated mass below, some of which expands, rises up the pipe, overflows and reduces the pressure even further. There comes a point at which the pressure of the rapidly expanding hot water at the base of the pipe is greater than the weight of water above it in the pipe. When this point is reached the superheated water begins to boil at an ever-increasing rate until it eventually 'flashes' into steam. This causes a high pressure explosion which blows the pipe's contents out in a spectacular fountain of boiling water. The pipe now starts to refill with water from the ground around the pipe and the cycle begins again.

Geysers eventually die, as their feeder channels become blocked by deposition of calcium carbonate on their walls, or by earthquake movements. An earthquake in 1953 caused the death of several geysers in Yellowstone, but it also created new ones.

CHAPTER THREE

EARTH MOVEMENTS

Earthquake zones coincide closely with those of volcanoes, for both are caused by movements in the unstable crust of our planet. But while all volcanic eruptions are accompanied by numerous small earthquakes, not all earthquakes are accompanied by volcanic eruptions. The reason for this is that when magma moves through the crust it must fracture rocks to do so, and when rocks fracture an earthquake occurs.

The Earth is made up of three main concentric shells. In the centre is the core, which is partly solid and partly plastic-liquid. Surrounding the core is the mantle, a thick shell composed largely of a rock called peridotite, which is rich in iron and magnesium. The mantle in turn is surrounded by the crust. The crust varies in thickness from 8km to 40km. It is broken into several plates, like a cracked eggshell. There are six large plates and six smaller ones, plus many smaller fragments. Some plates are parts of continents, such as Eurasia, Africa and America. Others lie under the oceans.

From radiometric dating we know that the Earth was formed as a mass of molten matter some 4,600 million years ago. Since that time

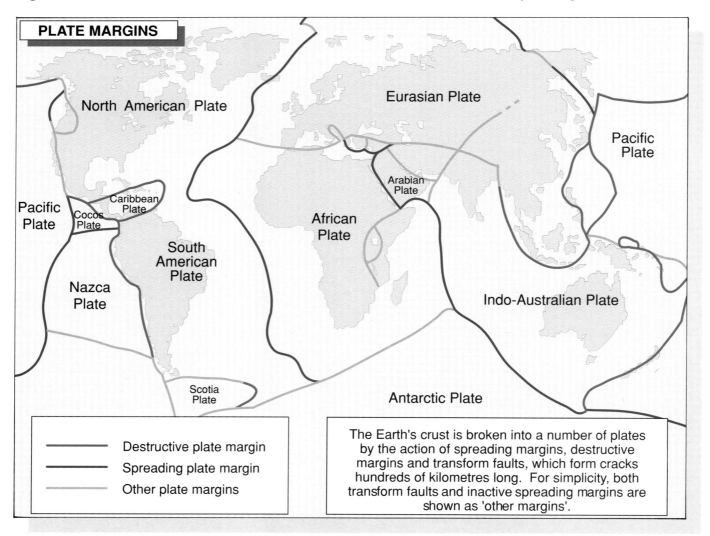

PLATE MARGINS

North American Plate

Eurasian Plate

Pacific Plate

Pacific Plate

Caribbean Plate

Cocos Plate

Arabian Plate

African Plate

South American Plate

Nazca Plate

Indo-Australian Plate

Scotia Plate

Antarctic Plate

— Destructive plate margin
— Spreading plate margin
— Other plate margins

The Earth's crust is broken into a number of plates by the action of spreading margins, destructive margins and transform faults, which form cracks hundreds of kilometres long. For simplicity, both transform faults and inactive spreading margins are shown as 'other margins'.

Mountain ranges such as the Himalayas (above) and the Alps were created when continental plates collided.

our planet has been cooling as heat is slowly lost to the surface. But in the asthenosphere, a layer in the upper mantle, certain elements produce additional heat. This heat is sufficient to partially melt mantle rock, which circulates in currents. The partially melted rock forms a platform on which the crustal plates 'float', and are carried around the surface of the world. When these moving plates meet and slide past each other, they generate earthquakes.

Plate tectonics

The edges of crustal plates are called plate margins. In some places, volcanic activity at plate margins leads to new crust being formed. Volcanic activity on the floor of the Atlantic, for example, is making the ocean bigger. In places, fresh magma pushes up from the mantle through the crust, and cools as it comes into contact with cold sea water. As it cools, it forms solid rock and creates new crust at the edge of the plate. These edges are known as spreading plate margins.

Spreading plate margins are part of the theory of plate tectonics, which was developed in 1969. This theory explains not only how new ocean floor is being created, but also how ancient crust is destroyed, along destructive plate margins.

If new crust was created but old crust was never destroyed, then of course the Earth would gradually get bigger. This does not happen because in some places, along destructive plate margins, oceanic crust is destroyed.

When continental and oceanic plates collide, one plate is destroyed. Convection currents drag the oceanic plate under the continental plate and back into the mantle, where it melts.

Plate margins in collision

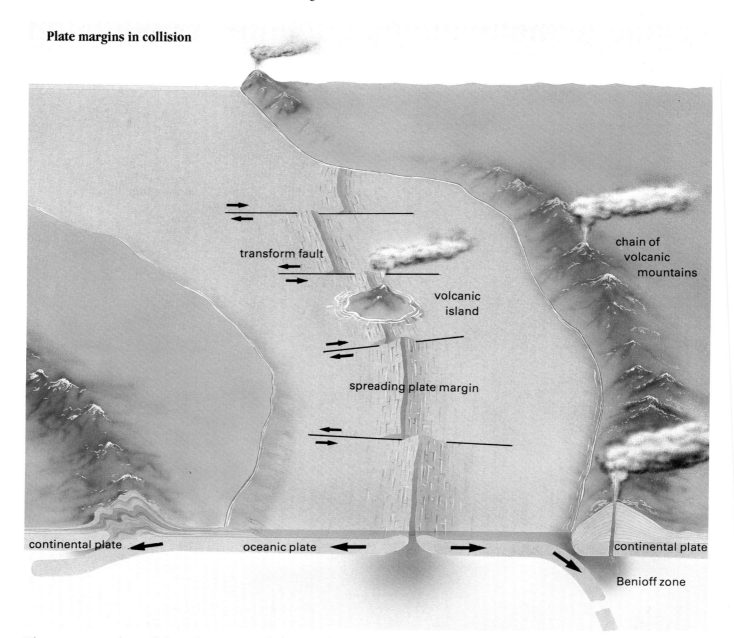

When an oceanic plate collides with a continental plate it is dragged under the land, along a line called the Benioff zone. Earthquakes occur as the oceanic plate scrapes against the continental plate. The collision of the plates also produces magma, as rocks in the Benioff zone melt. The magma rises through the continental plate to create volcanic mountains. Where two continental plates collide, sediments on the land are squeezed up to create mountains. On the sea bed, spreading plate margins form ridges where magma rises to the surface. Volcanic islands may form along the ridge and earthquakes occur along transform faults.

As the oceanic plate descends, along what is called a Benioff zone, it slides and scrapes against the underside of the continental plate, causing earthquakes. At the same time the intense pressure of the collision causes rock in the Benioff zone to melt and form magma. This magma is less dense than the surrounding rock and rises through the edge of the continental plate to the surface, to form chains of coastal volcanoes such as the Andes in South America and the Cascades in North America.

Scattered along the western margin of the Pacific Ocean are numerous curved chains of islands. These island arcs form where ocean crust is being destroyed by colliding oceanic plates. Here, the deep sea trenches at the Benioff zones fill with sea floor sediments. As one plate plunges to destruction in the mantle, it causes earthquakes and volcanism in the newly-forming volcanic islands above. The islands of Japan, the Philippines and Indonesia were created in this way and the people there live constantly under the threat of earthquakes and volcanic eruptions.

Hot spots

Streams of hot magma, called mantle plumes, rise up in places from the mantle and play on the underside of moving crustal plates. This produces a hot spot.

Sometimes the mantle plumes penetrate right through the crust and form volcanic islands such as Hawaii, and continental volcanoes such as Nyiragongo, Africa.

It was originally believed that these plumes came from deep inside the Earth's mantle, but recent research has indicated that they form in the asthenosphere.

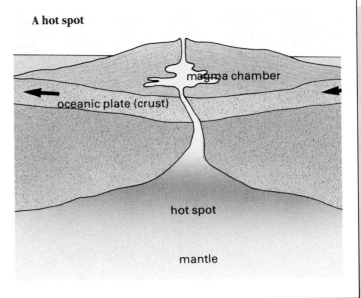

A hot spot

magma chamber

oceanic plate (crust)

hot spot

mantle

Vents on the sea floor along the East Pacific Rise release springs of very hot water (about 350°C). Sulphides make the water dark, and build up into 'chimneys', so these springs are known as black smokers.

Island arcs have been the site of some of the largest volcanic eruptions known: the 1883 eruption of Krakatoa in Indonesia (see page 6) and the 1902 eruption of Mt Pelée in the Caribbean (see page 42).

Earthquakes take place mostly at plate margins where they slide past each other, along transform faults. Transform faults form where spreading plate margins are producing new crust at different rates. The faults are cracks that form to accommodate this uneven growth.

Rocks do not slide smoothly along transform faults. The friction of them pressing together causes them to stick and jam. When these sticking rocks break apart, they do so with explosive force and produce earthquakes. It was the sudden movement along such faults that destroyed the cities of Lisbon, Portugal in 1757 and San Francisco, USA in 1906 (see page 26).

One of the most famous faults is the San Andreas Fault in California, USA, which is really a series of faults. They were formed by a movement along a Pacific Ocean spreading axis, known as the East Pacific Rise, part of which has pushed itself under the American continental plate and now disturbs the land above it as it forms new crust.

The San Andreas earthquakes are generated by two mechanisms: firstly by movement along the main fault itself, and secondly by movement along smaller faults as the disturbed blocks of crust resettle into position.

CHAPTER FOUR

EARTHQUAKES IN CLOSE-UP

Testing the tremors

Earthquakes send vibrations through the Earth. The vibrations spread out in the same way as ripples on a pond when a pebble is dropped into the water. In the pond we see only the vibrations that travel outwards as waves on the water's surface, but the vibrations also spread out beneath the surface in three dimensions.

Exactly the same thing takes place when rigid rocks near the surface of the Earth break suddenly. Vibrations known as waves spread out from the point of fracture (called the focus). The point on the ground immediately above the focus is called the epicentre and it is here that the waves first strike the surface. Some waves then travel outwards from the epicentre as surface waves and do not penetrate the crust deeply. Others travel inside the earth away from the focus.

The time of arrival of these wave vibrations is recorded on a seismometer. This is a sensitive instrument in which a complex pendulum assembly (seismogram) is able to record movement on a slowly rotating drum to give an earthquake trace (seismograph).

When rock breaks and produces shock waves, the waves travel through the Earth's crust and cause the ground at the surface to crack, break up and subside. When this happens, buildings collapse, gas and water mains fracture, flooding occurs as rivers and lakes overflow and giant waves (tsunami) are produced at sea.

While some earthquakes last only a few minutes, others may continue for days or weeks, with aftershocks taking place over a month or so. These drawn-out seismic events are often due to the first earthquake disturbing the structure of the surrounding countryside and breaking it up into blocks. These blocks often take several weeks to settle back into position and every movement they make causes a new earthquake.

The Mercalli scale

0 Movement registered only by seismographs.

1 Felt by only a few people, perhaps lying on hard ground.

2 Felt by people in bed, especially in tall buildings.

3 Felt by many people indoors. Hanging objects begin to swing.

4 Felt generally indoors. Parked cars rock, crockery rattles, walls crack.

5 Felt indoors and outside. Some people awakened. Objects fall over, trees shake. Some glass may break. At this level the vibrations and noises are for the first time recognised as an earthquake.

6 Felt by all. Furniture moves. Roof tiles fall. Difficult to walk.

7 Everyone hurries outside. Difficult to stand up. Buildings start to collapse – light damage in well-built buildings, but serious damage in poorly-constructed ones.

8 Panic. Difficult to drive. Factory chimneys, monuments and walls fall down. All windows break. Tree branches break. Cracks appear in the ground, and sand and mud spurt out. The level and temperature of water in wells changes.

9 General panic. Most buildings collapse partially or totally. Large cracks appear in the ground.

10 Dams break, flooding from lakes and rivers. Landslides. Railway lines twisted.

11 Underground pipes break. Few or no buildings survive. Valleys fill with mud from landslides or are flooded.

12 Total disaster. Towns razed to the ground. Large waves in the ground. Objects thrown into the air. Uncontrollable panic.

Earthquakes are measured by several means. The most common, and most scientific, is the Richter scale. This shows the total energy of a quake and is calculated from information gathered from seismometers. It is an open-ended scale, with each unit on the scale being 30 to 35 times greater than the one below it: 7 on this scale is a major quake and 8 is rarely surpassed, though the 1755 Lisbon quake did reach 8.9 Richter.

Where seismometers are not available, other, simpler and cheaper forms of measurement are used which rely on what is felt and seen by people in the affected area. Mercalli, for example, devised a scale which ranges from pottery being thrown into the air to wave movements in the ground. Twelve on the Mercalli Scale records a catastrophic disaster, in which cities are totally destroyed, the ground is seen to rise and fall in huge waves and total panic is induced in the population.

An earthquake that measured more than 5 on the Richter scale caused these tracks of the Northern Pacific Railway to collapse, and (inset) an 8.6 tremor damaged road and rail bridges in Alaska.

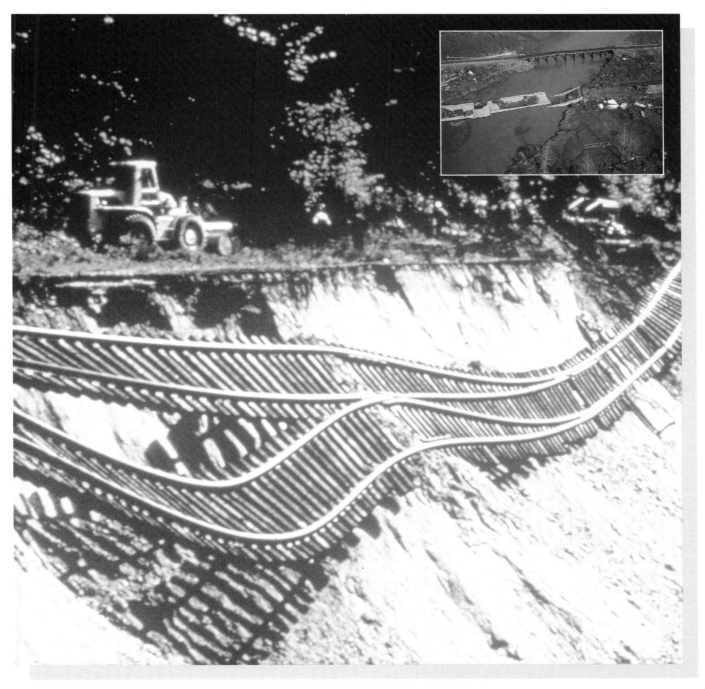

Huge tsunamis wreaked havoc along the southern coast of Alaska during the 1964 earthquake, one of the largest ever recorded. Ships were swept ashore at the port of Seward (above) and most of those who died were probably killed by the giant waves.

A tsunami rushes up a river in Hawaii, in 1946.

Waves of destruction

Earthquakes on the ocean floor produce tsunamis. Tsunamis are often — and wrongly — called tidal waves, although they have nothing to do with tides. These giant waves can cause untold

death and destruction along densely populated low-lying coasts. In 1892 a tsunami struck Japan, sweeping away around 10,000 houses and killing some 27,000 people. It was the giant tsunamis associated with the 1883 eruption of Krakatoa that were mainly responsible for the enormous death toll along the shores of Indonesia.

In the deep water found in the open ocean tsunamis pass almost unnoticed, but as they approach shallow water they change dramatically. On a gently sloping shore their height grows from one or two metres seen at sea into waves that may reach over 30m in height. Most of them are only six metres to 18m high, but even these can grow into mountains of water when channelled into a narrowing inlet.

When tsunamis arrive at the coast, the first wave is generally no worse than that of a heavy swell. This is followed by a rapid withdrawal of water from the coast as the trough behind the first waves arrives. Then the major wave arrives, carrying all before it and often sweeping deep inland. The lull before the next wave can last up to one hour and it is during such lulls that people have returned to salvage their possessions, only to be caught and killed by the waves that follow.

Camping in Hawaii

On 29 November 1975, the largest earthquake for a century shook the island of Hawaii. Early in the morning the first shock wave awoke most of the people, including 32 who were camping near Kalapana at Halape beach. This shock caused rock-falls from a hill near the campsite and several campers shifted their tents away from the hill and closer to the beach, then went back to bed.

An hour later an earthquake of 7.2 on the Richter scale struck the area. The ground disturbance was severe. The campers woke up, but found they were unable to stand. Within minutes of the shock the first tsunami arrived. This was soon followed by the second giant wave, washing people, trees and rocks into a crack six metres deep. One survivor described the experience as 'like being inside a giant washing machine'.

This second tsunami was about 15m high and travelled inland for nearly 100m. Some of the campers died, and there was considerable damage caused to property. The epicentre of this quake was below Kalapana and it caused a small volcanic eruption.

Death in China

Earthquake records in China date back to around 1100 BC and are fairly accurate from 780 BC onwards. In 1556 an earthquake of tremendous proportions struck Hsiän, in the province of Shensi. Most of the population there lived in caves dug in the soft rock of the surrounding hills. Most of these people were buried as their homes collapsed on them when the quake struck.

Floods ravaged the countryside as rivers were diverted from their courses, or formed lakes behind temporary landslide dams, which later burst. Famine and disease quickly followed, killing thousands. The official death toll, caused directly and indirectly by this earthquake, was set at 830,000.

In 1976, China was devastated by yet another large earthquake, which measured 7.2 on the Richter scale. The official death toll for this quake, which affected the Tsiensin province, was given as 650,000. The true death toll may never be known, but could exceed that of the 1556 quake.

Avalanche in Peru

In 1971 Señor Casaverde and some friends were visiting Yungay, in Peru. Yungay lies at the foot of a snow-covered mountain. They were driving past the village when Señor Casaverde's car began to shake.

'I stopped and got out to investigate, only to realise that an earthquake was taking place. I looked towards the village and saw several buildings collapse. About half a minute later I heard a tremendous roar from the nearby mountain and saw a huge cloud of dust rising from its upper slopes.'

The earthquake had fractured a large mass of rock and ice off the glacier on the north side, which was now crashing down a gorge towards the villages at the foot of the mountain. Señor Casaverde and his friends began to run towards Cemetery Hill, the only nearby patch of high ground. As they were climbing the hill, one of his friends fell. Stopping to help her he was horrified to observe a high wave of mud and rock was almost upon them. He recalls:

'The top of the wave was curved over like an enormous breaker crashing in from the ocean and was at least 79m high. Hundreds of the people of Yungay were running around in blind panic. The deafening roar was really terrifying. I reached the upper part of the hill just in time, as the debris avalanche hit the lower slopes. My friends and I must have saved ourselves by only 10 seconds. Lower down the hill I saw a man carrying two children who, as the wave hit him, threw the children to safety. Both the man, and two women near him, were swept away.'

The village of Yungay and several nearby villages were completely swept away. As many as 800,000 people were made homeless and 50,000 killed.

Devastation in America

In 1906 San Francisco was shaken by an earthquake lasting only 48 seconds, but during this brief time it caused damage calculated at 1000 million dollars (1906 values) and killed 700 people. All over the city, theatres, hotels and factories collapsed.

Fractured gas mains caught fire and the flames soon spread to the timbered buildings all over the city. These fires were so severe that the fire services had to use high explosives to create fire breaks. Even then, the fires raged for two days. Martial law was declared and thousands were made homeless.

The 1906 San Francisco earthquake ran along the San Andreas fault. Wooden buildings survived better than those built of brick or stone, but suffered in the fires that followed.

In 1964 an earthquake of 8.6 Richter struck Prince William Sound, Alaska, in the USA. At 5.30 pm a series of violent shocks, lasting just over four minutes, started landslides and avalanches. The ground rose or collapsed over an area of 207,000 sq km. More than 100 people were killed. Anchorage, 161km from the epicentre, was badly affected. Buildings swayed, toppled and were swallowed by huge cracks, along with trees and cars. An entire housing estate slid 500m downhill, ending up as a broken tangle of homes, trees, cars and telegraph poles. Tsunamis seven metres high swept along the coast of Alaska, and 4000km away the waves were still nearly as high and caused devastation along the beaches of California.

Many buildings collapsed during landsliding in Alaska in 1964.

CHAPTER FIVE

ENERGY FROM THE EARTH

Buried heat

When volcanoes erupt they can cause massive destruction, but the heat inside the Earth can be used positively. Electricity can be generated using steam produced by hot rocks deep underground. Geothermal energy is clean, it does not pollute the atmosphere and in many parts of the world it is abundant. Deep below the Earth's surface rocks, especially granites, are hotter the deeper they are. Granitic masses, and the hot ground that lies above magma chambers, can provide a constant source of geothermal energy. Even big lava flows can be tapped for their heat energy before they finally cool.

Geothermal power is produced by first drilling deep boreholes into hot rock. Water is pumped down to the rocks and circulated over them. The heat turns the water to steam, which is piped to the surface and used to drive turbines to generate electricity.

Hot water in Iceland: pipes carrying steam from boreholes to a geothermal power station and (inset) bathing in hot water from the nearby geothermal power station.

In Iceland, grapes, bananas
and exotic flowers can be
grown in greenhouses
heated by geothermal steam.

In Iceland, a geothermal power station provides 15,000 kilowatts of electricity per year, which is equivalent to 5000 electric heaters running at full power for twelve months. In Reykjavik, the capital, many homes are heated by hot water which is pumped from the Earth's underground heat bank. Just outside the city, glasshouses are heated by geothermal steam, enabling flowers, salad vegetables and even bananas to be grown.

The first commercial geothermal power station was built at Larderello, in Italy in 1905. It now produces 300 megawatts of electricity per year. Other successful geothermal power stations are now in operation at Wairakei in New Zealand (which produces 200,000 kilowatts of electricity a year), and at Geysers in the USA, which produces 13,000 kilowatts of electricity a year. Smaller geothermal schemes are now in use in countries such as Japan, Mexico and Chile. Even the thick lava flow produced by the 1973 eruption on Heimaey, in Iceland, has heat exchangers installed on it to provide low cost central heating for the next decade or so.

Geothermal power extraction is, however, not without its problems. For example, the water that is pumped into the hot ground can become contaminated with various chemicals and acids. This happened in Larderello, where the water corroded the generator turbine blades. The system had to be redesigned, so that the contaminated steam from the borehole is used to heat a secondary boiler, which contains acid-free water. The steam from this secondary boiler is clean and does not corrode the expensive turbine blades. The steam from the borehole is eventually condensed to provide a cheap source of boric acid (used in glass-making) and ammonia (used in fertilisers).

Volcanoes themselves contain vast reserves of heat energy just waiting to be tapped to provide cheap electricity, but there are obvious dangers. Within the past decade pilot schemes have been set up, using heat exchangers to extract this natural energy source. In a heat exchange system, water is pumped on to hot rocks and heated to produce steam, which rises to the surface to turn generators. Although still in its experimental stage and fraught with difficulties, the system does promise hopes for the future.

Metals from magma

Many of the metals that we use today are collected from around the top of magma bodies. Fluids from the magma are rich in dissolved metals. When magma invades the crust through cracks and fissures it cools to form rich veins of metal ore. Smaller amounts of metal ores are also found in the magma body itself and these may repay the cost of their extraction from recently cooled lava flows.

Copper, lead, tin, tungsten, uranium and sulphur are some of the valuable ores mined from around ancient magma bodies. Large quantities of copper come from the USA, tin comes from Malaya, lead and tin from the UK and tungsten and uranium from Czechoslovakia, Canada and the USA. Sulphur is mined in Sicily and in Chile. Precious metals such as gold, silver and platinum are mined in the USSR, USA, Mexico, Africa and South America. Diamonds

A church in Peru built of blocks of a volcanic rock called ignimbrite (see page 31)

are extracted from peridotite, a hard volcanic rock formed deep down where the very high pressures allow the carbon to crystallise and form the precious stone.

Buildings materials

Lava is quarried for roadstone in many countries throughout the world and, when crushed and mixed with pitch (a natural oil residue) forms the black sticky tarmacadam that is used to resurface roads. Ignimbrite (see page 14) and pozzulana (a similar material found in Italy) are soft enough to be cut into bricks, yet firm enough to be used for building. In Peru, Italy and the Canary Islands houses and churches are constructed of these rocks.

Ash-fall deposits, such as pumice and tephra, are used in a variety of products. Pumice, although sold in blocks for cleaning steps, or removing hard skin from the feet, is mostly crushed into powders of varying fineness. The coarser grades are used as industrial and domestic abrasives, while the finest have been used in cosmetics and in toothpaste! In the Canary Islands, pumice is widely used in agriculture. Farmers spread pumice fragments on their fields to a depth of 30cm or so. Pumice is a good insulator so it stops the soil drying out in the hot sun, while its fine cavities trap the nightly falls of dew.

In prehistoric times many cultures used obsidian (volcanic glass) to make arrowheads, spearheads and various cutting tools. Obsidian is still used in parts of Mexico to make ornaments for sale to tourists.

Because obsidian can be knapped, broken into shapes with razor sharp edges or into sharp slivers, it was of great value to many cultures and was traded across continents. Obsidian fragments discovered by archaeologists provide clues to ancient trade routes across Europe and America.

In Tenerife, the volcanic soil is farmed in terraces, and (inset) pumice is spread up to 40cm thick to reduce water loss.

CHAPTER SIX

DAMAGE AND PREDICTION

After an earthquake

It is difficult to imagine the scale of damage both immediate and long-term, that an earthquake or volcanic eruption can cause. Severe ground vibrations during earthquakes cause walls to crack and buildings to collapse; badly designed or poorly constructed ones are most at risk. Communications break down: roads crack, railway lines break, power lines and telephone lines are cut. Dams may burst and cause terrible flooding. Essential services such as power and drinking water are cut off. Medical supplies to combat the disease that often follows are always in short supply. During earthquakes most people die either by being hit by falling masonry when buildings collapse, or by drowning when dams burst. But the indirect effects such as famine and disease can cause even greater loss of life.

Tsunamis are major indirect hazards, particularly on highly populated low-lying coastlines. They have been known to sweep away entire villages, together with their inhabitants. Earthquakes may also trigger avalanches of mud, snow and ice, which bury people alive.

After a volcanic eruption

Volcanic hazards are caused by ash-falls, ash-flows, mudflows and lava flows. Lava flows rarely kill, but they can damage buildings and land. Large ash-falls are like heavy snow falls and can bury towns and villages under thick layers of volcanic ash which, near the volcano, can reach over six metres. The fall of heavy rock fragments can injure and kill. During the 1971 eruption of Mt Etna in Sicily, a team of French volcanologists left three reinforced helmets stacked together outside overnight. In the morning it was found that a rock thrown out by the volcano had penetrated right through all three helmets; the rock fragment was no larger than five centimetres.

Ash-flows are rapidly moving clouds of red-hot volcanic dust. The intense blast that accompanies them pushes people, animals and buildings over, and the red-hot dust incinerates and buries all in its path. A prehistoric ash-flow in Japan crossed mountains 670m high and travelled 64km while in 1902 a small flow of this type wiped out St Pierre in Martinique, killing over 30,000 (see page 42).

An earthquake in Guatemala destroys homes.

Lava sets fire to grass and scrub in Hawaii.

When a volcano on the island of Heimaey, Iceland, erupted people sprayed the lava with sea water for several months to try to halt its flow.

Bombing lava flows

Some attempts have been made to divert lava flows away from buildings and farmland. Explosives have been used to make an opening in the side of the main lava flow to allow the lava to follow a different course. The idea of bombing a lava flow to change its course is based on the idea that thin, runny pahoehoe lava can be converted into a thick pasty aa lava by breaking up its hardened surface with explosives (see page 13). The aa lava thus created would move only slowly, create an effective barrier to the more fluid lava behind, cause it to spill out sideways and form lateral flows along other routes. In 1935 the US Air Corps bombed a lava flow during an eruption on the island of Hawaii. The results of this exercise were not conclusive, but at least opened the way for further experimentation. A more effective, and cheaper, way to breach a lava flow may be to use heavy artillery fire. The breach could be kept open with repeated shelling. This, like other diversion systems, will only work providing the topography is suitable, that is, if there is somewhere for the lava to flow where it will cause less damage than along its original path.

Protective clothing

The greatest dangers during volcanic eruptions are falling debris and thick, suffocating dust. A protective helmet or even a hat stuffed with newspaper can prevent head injuries. Thick wool pullovers and anoraks protect the body against falling debris. Dust may be filtered out by breathing through a damp cloth. Volcanologists wear thick aluminium-coated suits to reflect the intense heat when working close to hot lava flows. Special masks and respirators are also used to filter out gas and dust.

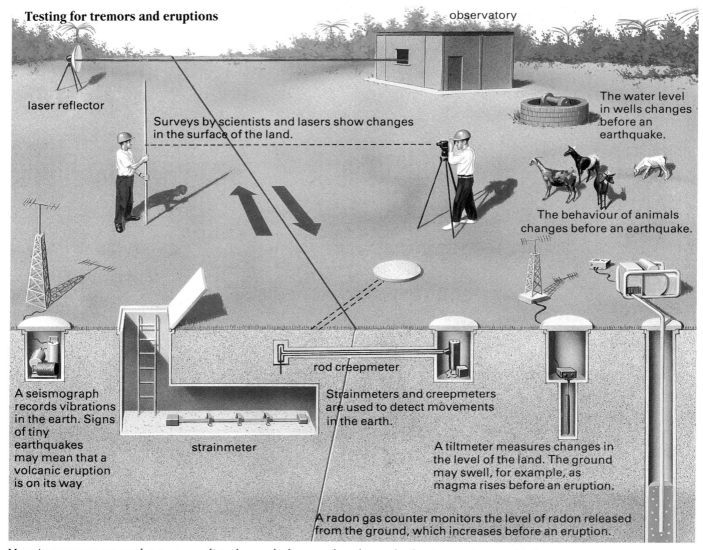

Testing for tremors and eruptions

observatory

laser reflector

Surveys by scientists and lasers show changes in the surface of the land.

The water level in wells changes before an earthquake.

The behaviour of animals changes before an earthquake.

A seismograph records vibrations in the earth. Signs of tiny earthquakes may mean that a volcanic eruption is on its way

strainmeter

rod creepmeter

Strainmeters and creepmeters are used to detect movements in the earth.

A tiltmeter measures changes in the level of the land. The ground may swell, for example, as magma rises before an eruption.

A radon gas counter monitors the level of radon released from the ground, which increases before an eruption.

Many instruments are used to try to predict when and where earthquakes and volcanic eruptions are likely to occur.

Detecting disaster

Over the past 20 years it has become clear that for most parts of the world there is not enough evidence to permit earthquakes to be predicted with any great accuracy. The science of earthquake prediction is still in its infancy. Much of the research to improve our ability to forecast when and where quakes will take place is being done by seismologists in Japan, China and the USA, some of the countries most at risk from seismic events. But prediction is expensive and needs costly instruments to monitor and detect any change in the physical properties of the crust. Information from them is fed, via telemetry (satellite communication), to a central laboratory for careful analysis.

Earthquake surveillance requires skilled scientists to interpret records and teams of technicians to service the instruments. Poor countries cannot afford such expensive round-the-clock surveillance and it is these countries that are most at risk. Predicting volcanic eruptions is as costly as predicting earthquakes, but is generally more successful. The three methods currently in use are geophysical, chemical and tephrochronological.

Geophysical techniques employ exactly the same methods as those used for earthquake prediction, for it is essential to locate precisely where rising magma is splitting rocks apart and causing small quakes. By carefully logging the movement of magma below the surface we can tell the direction in which it is moving, its speed of ascent and hopefully calculate when and where it will erupt.

Chemical prediction measures gases released by fumaroles on, or near volcanoes. The gases

Animal instincts

Recent research in animal behaviour has given some surprising results. Birds have inborn magnetic field detectors, while some animals are sensitive to extremely small vibrations and sound waves. This may explain why some animals are restless, or hurriedly leave areas just before an earthquake takes place. In 1976 a city in China was evacuated on the basis of such information, hours before an earthquake struck and reduced it to rubble.

A crowned pigeon

are collected in glass cylinders and analysed. Sulphur dioxide, carbon dioxide, hydrogen and radon gas increase just before eruption.

In geology it is said 'the present is the key to the past'. In the prediction of volcanic events the reverse is also true. Using the science of tephrochronology, geologists carefully map and record details of ash-fall deposits (tephra) from past eruptions. Analysis of their results tells us what kind of eruptions have taken place in the past, how long they lasted, how large were the areas affected and how long was the repose period between eruptions. This information helps scientists to predict future eruptions.

All these methods of prediction are so far used only on a research basis. Governments will not accept the high costs involved for random investigations of potentially dangerous volcanoes. Each volcano needs 900 man-hours of research work to provide meaningful results, which makes such an exercise too costly for those countries most at risk.

The science of prediction has told us a great deal about how quakes and volcanoes behave, and what type of event to expect next in a high risk area, but the science of prediction does not always allow us to say with any great degree of accuracy when an earthquake or eruption will next occur. For many places in the world it could be in a 1000 years or it could be tomorrow.

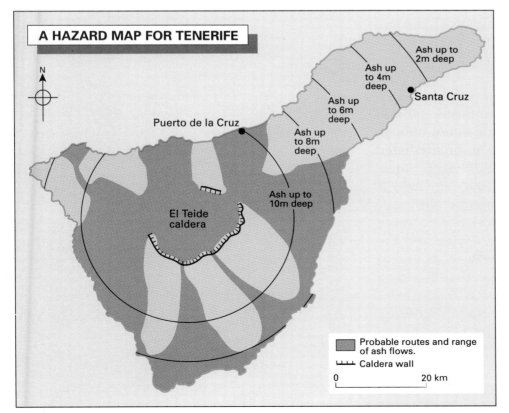

A HAZARD MAP FOR TENERIFE

N

Ash up to 2m deep

Ash up to 4m deep

Ash up to 6m deep

Santa Cruz

Ash up to 8m deep

Puerto de la Cruz

El Teide caldera

Ash up to 10m deep

Probable routes and range of ash flows.

Caldera wall

0   20 km

Scientists can predict where ash is most likely to flow, and how deep air-fall ash could be, on the island of Tenerife the next time El Teide erupts.

CHAPTER SEVEN

FOUNDATIONS FOR THE FUTURE

There is little we can do to prevent the enormous damage that can be caused by large scale natural disasters such as earthquakes and volcanic eruptions, but there is much that can be done to ensure that loss of life and damage to property is kept to a minimum.

Traditional buildings

The massive earthquake that struck Leninakan, in Armenia in 1988 left 40,000 people dead and many thousands homeless. Eighty per cent of the city was destroyed. In 1990 an earthquake in Iran killed 40,000 people and made about half a million homeless. Traditional housing in earthquake-prone parts of the world is often not designed to withstand the effects of such disasters and many people are killed as their homes collapse. Scientists and engineers around the world are carrying out research to find building materials and techniques that will survive the stresses that affect houses and multi-storey blocks during an earthquake.

In poor developing countries, where little money is available for high technology, it is obviously important to make full use of local materials and labour. Basic guidelines such as those for traditional houses in India show what could be done immediately to strengthen new buildings of mud and stone. They should be one storey high, since higher buildings are more liable to collapse. Rooms should not be more than 4.5 sq m and large rooms should have thicker walls. Door and window openings should be as small as possible, because such openings weaken walls. Roofs with sloping sides and ends are best because they put less stress on walls than other roof designs. Tie beams would help to hold walls together at the corners, and so on.

After the earthquake in Iran, the UN sent a team to the affected region to help set up a

reconstruction plan. The UN's aim was 'not to provide stronger houses but to help people build stronger houses. . . . In the future, earthquakes of the size and severity of the June 1990 earthquake must be ridden like a passing wave, with infrastructure and buildings strong enough to withstand them. One day, earthquakes in Iran should be natural events, not natural disasters.'

Many survivors of the 1988 Armenian earthquake were left homeless. Leninakan, 50km from the epicentre of the quake, was largely destroyed.

A tower that did not topple

The LatinAmericano Tower, built in 1956 in Mexico City, has 44 floors and is 181 m high. It was designed to avoid damage during earthquakes. The engineer in charge of the project was in his office on the 25th floor when a massive earthquake struck the city in 1985.

'I was sitting at my desk selecting photographs when I began to experience a minor movement. About five seconds later my chair suffered a large displacement of approximately 60 cm (my chair is on castors on a plastic sheet); all the pictures on the wall moved. I stood up and walked with difficulty to the corner of the room, looking south. Only eight seconds had passed from the first movement of the rocking action.

I saw through the window a building whose top four floors collapsed, a 27-storey building whose top six floors failed. I started to see, in different directions, clouds of dust indicating buildings collapsing. The movement was very large, so I went back to a column away from the window. The movement did not stop. It had no end . . .

Finally, three minutes after the first movement, the tower stopped. The earthquake was over! I started to worry about possible damage to the tower; the movement was very strong.'

In fact, the tower had suffered only minor damage – a few broken windows and cracking in some partition walls, for example – whereas buildings all round had collapsed to the ground.

Mexico City, after the 1985 earthquake

Modern buildings

Engineers are now confident that they can design buildings, bridges, dams or indeed any kind of structure so that they won't be a threat to life, even in the most severe earthquake. The experience of damage in recent earthquakes bears this out (see box).

An engineer designing a building in earthquake country first looks at the ground. Is there a chance that a surface fault may cross the site? If so, it is best to move elsewhere. For example, building is now prohibited to either side of parts of the San Andreas fault in California.

Another danger that needs to be investigated is when building on sandy soils, which may turn to quicksand when the ground shakes. This has caused many buildings to sink or tilt. Until 15 years ago, it was not fully understood when this might happen, but routine tests and analysis can now identify the problem soils. Having found the problem, there are various ways of dealing with it. For example, cement can be injected

The San Andreas fault – the fine dark line on the right of this picture – extends almost the length of California, in the USA.

into the sand, so that when the cement sets the soil is locked into a solid block which cannot turn into quicksand. Alternatively, the foundations can be extended down on to rock or other firm materials which do not pose a risk.

The third important danger is from soft soils, which sometimes shake and vibrate much more violently in an earthquake than firmer ground. The most famous example of this is the centre of Mexico City which is built on the very soft soils left by the bed of a dried-up lake. In the great 1985 Mexican earthquake, almost all the buildings which collapsed were on the lake bed, while the buildings on firmer ground nearby survived. If you must build on such dangerous soils, make sure your building has extra strength and resilience!

Having examined the dangers in the soil, the building itself must be made safe. Earthquake engineers generally allow their buildings to sway a great deal in a strong earthquake, like a branch shaken by a gale, but they must make sure the buildings can bend without snapping. Brittle buildings can't do this; they collapse, killing their occupants. Brick buildings tend to be brittle, but by adding steel rods between the bricks, engineers can make them much less liable to snap. Modern steel or reinforced concrete buildings can be made even more flexible and earthquake-resistant.

Designs for tomorrow's world

Recently, engineers have been developing other ways of combating earthquakes. One idea is to mount the building on rubber springs, which act like shock absorbers in a car, smoothing out the ride while the ground shakes. A number of buildings and bridges have now been built using this 'base isolation' technique.

The isolators work by reducing the earthquake energy transmitted to the building. They allow it to move gently several centimetres to the left and right during an earthquake instead of very violently. The isolators may be square or round, about 75cm across by 50cm high. They are made of a sandwich of thick layers of rubber and thin steel plates. The system has already been used in more than 200 buildings and bridges around the world; most of these structures are in Japan, the USA and New Zealand.

The technique is particularly useful for protecting buildings like hospitals, communications centres and emergency centres during an earthquake, since they play such an important role in disaster recovery. Although the base isolation method is a bit more expensive, it pays

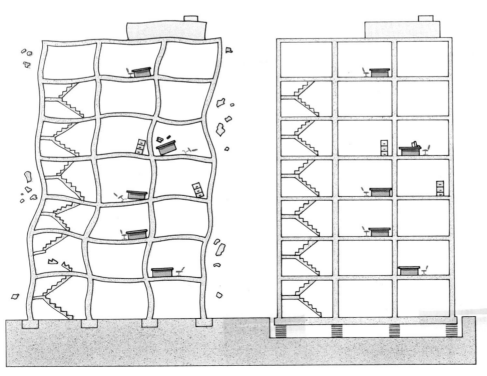

Buildings on normal foundations (far left) bend and break up during earthquakes. Buildings on base isolators (left) move horizontally at floor level during an earthquake: the building, its occupants and contents are protected from the effect of the tremor.

for itself many times over after the building has survived its first quake.

Even more sophisticated buildings are now being planned, using space age technology. In one system, computers are used to sense the movements of a building; steel ropes are then slackened or tightened to pull the building back into shape.

These new methods are being used more and more for valuable buildings in city centres. However, the older tried and trusted ways of providing strength and ductility will still continue to protect the vast majority of buildings in earthquake country for many years to come.

Testing time

An engineer designing a building or bridge in earthquake country needs to check, *before* construction starts, that it really will be able to stand up to violent ground shaking. Usually, this will involve an analysis using a computer; the new generation of high-speed computers and sophisticated programs means that quite accu-

rate predictions can be made as to how a structure will behave in an earthquake. Sometimes the mathematical models of a structure using a computer need to be backed up by more direct tests. A building or bridge is too big and expensive to build and test in a laboratory, so engineers tend to do one of two things. They may make just one or two critical parts of the building, for example a critical beam or column. Then they push this critical part backwards and forwards in a testing machine to see if it can stand up to the swaying of an earthquake. Or they make a model of the complete building and mount it on an earthquake 'shaking table'. These shaking tables are programmed to rock and lurch around, tracking the motions recorded during actual earthquakes. Shaking table tests can be an excellent way of checking out new and unusual designs, long before any money is spent on building the structure itself.

A model of a 10-storey building is tested on an earthquake shaking table (below left) and a computer produces a drawing (below) to show the effects.

Shelters against volcanoes

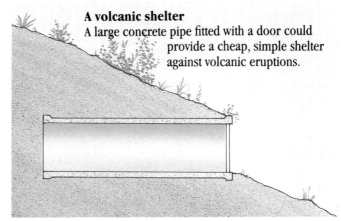

A volcanic shelter
A large concrete pipe fitted with a door could provide a cheap, simple shelter against volcanic eruptions.

The course of volcanic eruptions are predictable. Lava flows, mudflows and small nuée ardentes (red-hot clouds of gas and volcanic ash) keep to valleys and low lying ground. While ash-falls near the volcano are dangerous, those at some distance from it are not, although buildings will collapse unless ash is constantly cleared from flat or gently sloping roofs. For this reason buildings must be constructed with steeply sloping roofs to minimise roof collapse, while valleys and low-lying ground should be avoided when siting new villages near dangerous volcanoes.

While large-scale nuées will fill small valleys and overflow over the surrounding countryside, there is a simple way of protecting people even from these clouds of destruction. A few days before the 1902 eruption of Mont Pelée, Martinique, Augustus Cyparis was imprisoned in the town jail in St. Pierre. The jail is solidly built of thick stone and it saved his life when 30,000 people around him died. After he was rescued he was pardoned and he earned his living by travelling with a circus and exhibiting his burns.

Shelters similar to Cyparis's prison could be provided easily and cheaply by using large concrete pipes, about 2m in diameter, like those used for sewers. Such pipes buried in hillsides, close to villages, would provide adequate shelter for people during a nueé ardente eruption.

The stone prison (inset) that saved Cyparis from the nuée ardente that rushed down the slopes of Mont Pelée (below).

Rescue workers at the scene of the 1989 earthquake in San Francisco, USA, and (inset) local miners searching the ruins of a hotel that collapsed during a quake in the Philippines in 1990. They rescued someone found alive after being trapped for two and a half weeks.

Search and rescue

Although large buildings can, where funds allow, be made earthquake resistant, housing in earthquake-prone regions is unlikely ever to match the same standards. Search and rescue operations will continue to be a vital role of local authorities and aid organisations.

In Armenia, more than 40,000 people were trapped in collapsed buildings after the 1988 earthquake. People trapped in this way need to be rescued quickly if they are to survive. About 90 per cent of people found alive under rubble are rescued on the first day after a quake. Search and rescue teams use all kinds of equipment to find victims, from infrared detectors to carbon dioxide sensors, but the scale of such disasters often makes it impossible to reach everyone in time. Experts believe that more lives could be saved if rescuers understood more about how particular types of buildings collapse. V-shaped spaces, for example, offer one of the best chances of survival, so rescuers need to find those spaces first.

The people of Japan have often experienced natural disasters such as earthquakes, and have learnt a great deal about how to deal with the aftermath of such events. Their government has now set up disaster relief teams to help other countries stricken by disaster. The teams are ready to leave at very short notice and are equipped with instruments that help to find, rescue and treat disaster victims, from acoustic ground detectors and thermal imaging cameras to rock drills. Warehouses in Japan and abroad are stocked with blankets, tents, electricity generators, equipment to purify drinking water, communication devices and medical supplies.

More and more countries, from Iceland to Italy and Canada to New Zealand, are training dogs to help find people buried after natural disasters. The scheme was started by a Swiss who trained dogs to find people trapped by avalanches, and organisations have now been set up round the world to assist in rescue work following earthquakes and similar disasters.

A goal for the 1990s

During the last 20 years natural disasters, such as earthquakes and floods, have killed about three million people. Whilst such disasters cannot usually be prevented, much could be done to reduce the loss of life and damage to property. The United Nations has proclaimed the 1990s the 'International Decade for Natural Disaster Reduction'. Countries round the world are being asked to look at how best to plan for such disasters and how to use advances in science and technology to reduce their impact.

As part of the UN scheme several thousand people are to be trained in disaster relief work, and they in turn will travel to different parts of the world to train local people. It is hoped that projects such as the training programme will help countries in the developing world in particular, where the impact of natural disasters is usually far more devastating than in developed countries. For example, a recent earthquake in San Francisco, USA, which measured 7.5 on the Richter scale, killed about 100 people and hardly affected the economy of the country. But an earthquake of the same intensity in a developing country might kill 50,000 people and the economy might take 20 years to recover. It is only by cooperation on a global scale that this imbalance will be improved by the next century.

GLOSSARY

ash fall – rock blasted out of the vent of a volcano, which settles over the countryside like a blanket of snow.

ash flow – pumice and rock dust from a volcanic eruption, which is carried along while supported by high temperature gases. Such flows are capable of travelling at high speeds over great distances.

asthenosphere – a weaker layer of rocks beneath the brittle surface of the Earth that is able to flow and carry the continental plates around the surface of our planet.

Benioff zone – a steeply dipping zone where an oceanic plate is carried below a continental plate, where numerous earthquakes are generated and where rocks melt, causing volcanism on the edge of the overlying continental plate.

caldera – a large depression formed by the upper part of a volcano slowly collapsing into its own magma chamber as material is released during a large volcanic eruption.

epicentre – the point on the Earth's surface immediately above the focus of an earthquake.

fumarole – an opening in the ground from which gases are released.

hawaiian eruption – an eruption of thin runny lava from which gases can escape easily, characterised by spectacular fire fountains.

ignimbrite – volcanic rock, usually quite dense, that results from the collapse of a nuée ardente.

lava – molten rock that flows at the Earth's surface.

magma – molten rock that flows below the Earth's surface.

mantle – that part of the earth that lies between the crust (at the surface) and the core at the centre of the planet.

nuée ardente – red-hot clouds of gas and volcanic ash that rush across the ground (also called glowing avalanche).

plate – one of several large fragments that make up the Earth's surface.

plinian eruption – an eruption of great violence characterised by an intense gas blast which throws fragmented rock as high as 50km.

pyroclastic rock – fragmented rocks formed at high temperature. Non-pyroclastic rocks are so-called because they come from lava flows and not from material thrown out of the volcano.

rootless lava flow – a lava flow that begins where lava falls to the surface and that has no direct connection with molten rock below the surface.

strombolian eruption – an eruption of thick lava from which gas cannot escape easily.

transform fault – fault that forms in response to uneven generation of new crust at spreading plate margins.

INDEX

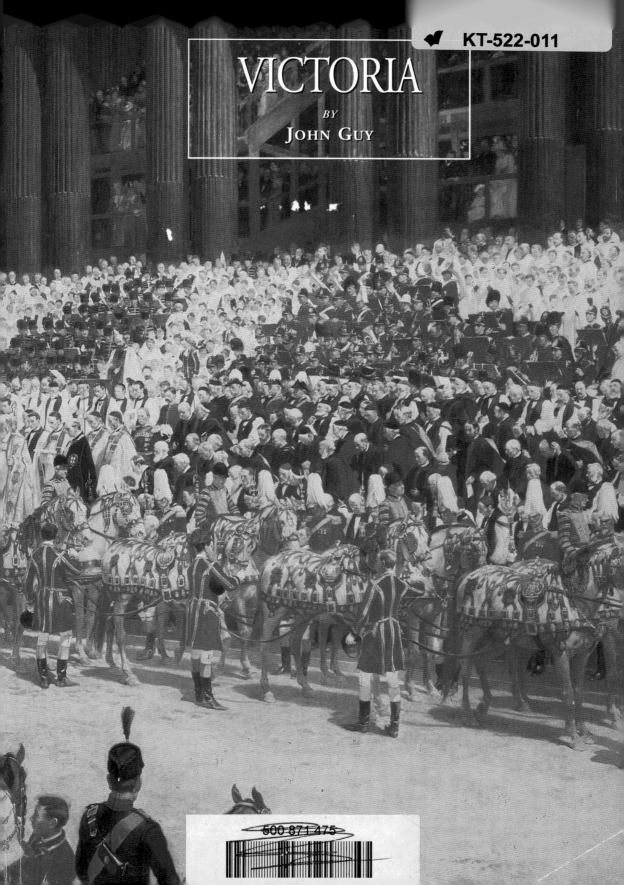

VICTORIA

BY
JOHN GUY

THE YOUNG VICTORIA

When Victoria was born on 24 May 1819 she was fifth in line to the throne and the likelihood of her succeeding seemed very remote. Her grandfather, George III, was still king and ahead of her in succession were her uncles, George, the Prince Regent, the Dukes of York and Clarence, and of course her father, the Duke of Kent. Within a short space of time, however, all that changed. Her father died unexpectedly on 23 January 1820 followed, six days later, by her grandfather. The Duke of York died in 1827, taking her a step nearer the throne. Her remaining uncles succeeded as George IV and William IV, respectively, but their failing health produced no heirs, leaving Victoria as heir to the throne.

VICTORIA IS BORN

Victoria was born at Kensington Palace and was christened exactly one month later in the Cupola Room at the Palace. There was a dispute over her name, her parents eventually settling on Alexandrina Victoria as her registered name, but they called her Victoria from birth.

PERSONAL POSSESSIONS

Many of Queen Victoria's personal possessions still survive, a number of them on view at the Victoria and Albert Museum. These reading glasses once belonged to the Queen; the case is inscribed with her personal insignia.

WILLIAM IV

Victoria's uncle, William IV, became King at the age of 64 on the death of his brother, and when he died in 1837 he left no legitimate heirs to the throne. Victoria became queen as his closest living relative.

THE YOUNG PRINCESS

Always a friendly and playful child (who had no fewer than 132 dolls!), she had an aptitude for music, singing and dancing and was an accomplished artist. She spoke with a strong German accent as a child, because of her mother's German origins, and she could speak German and French fluently.

THE QUEEN COMES OF AGE

Princess Victoria was just 18 years old when she heard of the death of her uncle, William IV, in 1837. She was immediately filled with feelings of both happiness and sadness, but seems to have assumed the awesome responsibility with apparent calm. She was crowned the following year, on 28 June, at Westminster Abbey. Not a popular figure at first, she was destined to become Britain's longest reigning monarch and ruler over the greatest empire the world has ever seen.

DUCHESS OF KENT

Victoria's father was Edward, Duke of Kent, fourth son of George III. Victoria never knew her father, who died when she was a baby. Her mother, the Duchess of Kent, was appointed Regent in case Victoria succeeded to the throne whilst still a child.

PRINCE ALBERT

O ne of the first dilemmas facing Victoria when she succeeded to the throne was that of marriage. Lord Melbourne, the Prime Minister, advised Victoria to marry as soon as possible to create her own heirs. At first she had no interest in doing so but agreed to meet her cousin, Prince Albert of Saxe-Coburg-Gotha. Both entered the relationship reluctantly at first, but there seems to have been a mutual attraction and they soon became very dear friends. After marriage their friendship developed into a very deep and genuine love for one another and they became a devoted couple.

THE PRINCE CONSORT

Prince Albert was, in Victoria's own words, *'so sensible, so kind, and so good, and so amiable…the most pleasing and delightful exterior and appearance you can possibly see.'* He was tall, intelligent and proved to be a very able political adviser to Victoria. He took a genuine interest in his new adoptive country, particularly the poorer classes. He is credited with re-introducing the practice of bringing decorated Christmas trees into the house, a custom still practised in his native Germany, though it had long fallen out of favour in England.

THE ROYAL WEDDING

The wedding between Victoria and Albert took place on 10 February 1840 at St. James's Palace. They were both just 20 years old. She wore a white satin gown with a lace flounce, and a Turkish diamond necklace and sapphire brooch (a present from Albert). The couple were well received by the public. After the wedding reception held at Buckingham Palace, they had a three-day honeymoon at Windsor Castle.

THE PRINCE DIES

In 1861 Prince Albert contracted typhoid and died prematurely, at the age of 42. The Queen was heartbroken. The prospect of facing the world alone culminated in a nervous breakdown. She wore black for the rest of her life in respect for Albert. At first the public sympathized with her, but after over a decade of mourning, there were calls for her abdication.

THE QUEEN PROPOSES

According to the dictates of royal protocol, no man is allowed to propose to a queen, so Victoria had to ask for Albert's hand in marriage. She proposed to him on 15 October 1839. In her diary, Victoria wrote that Albert's acceptance was the brightest and happiest moment of her life.

KEEPSAKES

To commemorate the royal wedding a great many mementoes were made, such as this decorative lustre-ware jug.

EVENTS OF VICTORIA'S LIFE

~1819~
Victoria born at Kensington Palace

~1820~
Victoria's father Edward, Duke of Kent, dies

~1830~
George IV dies

William IV accedes to the throne

~1832~
First Reform Act passed to reform parliamentary system

~1833~
Slavery abolished throughout the Empire

~1834~
Poor Law creates workhouses for the poor

Houses of Parliament burn down

~1837~
William IV dies

Victoria accedes to the throne

~1838~
Victoria's coronation

People's Charter issued, calling for political reform

~1839~
First camera developed

~1840~
Victoria marries Albert of Saxe-Coburg-Gotha

FAMILY LIFE

Victoria is often pictured as a stern, austere woman, an image perpetuated by her choice to wear black for so many years after Albert's death. She is seldom seen smiling in pictures, but supposedly was a jovial person. One reason for her glum expressions was possibly the slow film speed used by photographers at the time. Subjects often had to hold a pose for 30 seconds (or longer) so as not to blur the image, making it difficult to hold a smile. Historians have often concentrated on the more serious side to Victoria's personality, neglecting her love of life, particularly family life. She was amused by the antics of children and both she and Albert enjoyed simple, family pastimes. In later life, Victoria loved to see herself as the great matriarch.

SOFTLY, SOFTLY

Contrary to popular opinion, Victoria was not a strict authoritarian. She preferred to instruct her children by setting a good moral example rather than to over-discipline them.

THE GRANDMOTHER OF EUROPE

This picture, taken in 1897, shows the extended family of Queen Victoria. The Prince of Wales (and future king Edward VII) stands immediately to her left. By the various marriages of her children and grand-children, Victoria was related to all of the major royal houses of Europe, including Germany, Norway, Sweden, Greece, Spain, Romania and Russia, earning her the affectionate title 'the grandmother of Europe'.

HAPPY FAMILIES

In keeping with most families of the day, Victoria and Albert had many children, nine in all. She gave birth to Princess Victoria (Vicky) in November 1840. Vicky, the Princess Royal, remained a close friend throughout the Queen's life, especially after Albert's death. Victoria's family life was, by all accounts, a happy one. It is difficult to say what kind of relationship she had with all her children: some accounts claim she was aloof and dispassionate, others paint a rosier picture. There does appear to have been real animosity between her and Edward, the future king, whom she thought foolish, and was critical of his behaviour.

PERSONAL RECOLLECTIONS

We know a great deal about the personal life and opinions of Queen Victoria from her diary, which she maintained throughout her life. It was not, as many suppose, a secret diary, certainly not in her younger years, because it was frequently perused by her mother and governess.

~1840~
Penny postal service introduced

Princess 'Vicky' born (Victoria's first child)

~1841~
Sir Robert Peel becomes Prime Minister

~1845~
Beginning of Irish potato famine

~1846~
Corn Laws repealed

~1851~
Great Exhibition in London, initiated by Prince Albert

~1853~
Vaccination against smallpox made compulsory

Albert begins rebuilding Balmoral Castle to his own designs

~1854~
Crimean War breaks out between Britain (and France) and Russia

~1856~
Victoria Cross first introduced for bravery in wartime

~1857~
Indian Mutiny against British rule

ASSASSINATION ATTEMPTS

At the beginning of her reign Victoria was not a popular figure at all. As ruling monarch, she was often seen as the cause of social discontent; some would have preferred a king on the throne. There were several attempts made on Victoria's life including this attempt in 1840 by Edward Oxford.

REFORM ACTS

During her reign, Victoria approved several Acts of Parliament that had important social and constitutional implications. Growing unrest in Britain meant new political movements were forcing change. In 1838 the Chartists issued the 'Peoples' Charter' which called for political reform. Although not fully realized until 1944, it forms the basis of our parliamentary system today. In 1867 and 1884, the Second and Third Reform Acts extended the right to vote to more people.

FATHER FIGURE

During the early years of her reign Victoria relied heavily on the advice of Lord Melbourne, the Whig (Liberal) Prime Minister, who guided her through the intricacies of politics and her role in government.

SOCIAL CHANGE

The Industrial Revolution saw Britain change from a mainly agricultural nation to an industrial one. People who left the country to seek employment in the towns were exploited by greedy industrialists. Trade unionists like Joseph Arch, founder of the National Union of Farm Labourers (shown right), fought a long and hard battle for workers' rights. Trade unions were finally legalized in 1871.

VICTORIA & GOVERNMENT

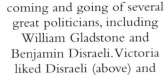

From the beginning Victoria showed a genuine interest in the government of the country and developed a good rapport with most of the leading politicians of the day. She took her role seriously and, whilst accepting the relatively new idea of a constitutional monarchy (which meant that she had no real part to play in politics), she also realized that she had considerable influence and exercised her powers wisely. Albert, who had shown little interest in politics prior to their marriage, also took an active role in matters of government.

POLITICAL GIANTS

Victoria witnessed the coming and going of several great politicians, including William Gladstone and Benjamin Disraeli. Victoria liked Disraeli (above) and had him invested Earl of Beaconsfield, whereas Gladstone frequently incurred her wrath.

A NEW HOUSE FOR PARLIAMENT

Until the reign of Victoria's uncle, William IV, Parliament met in the old royal palace of Westminster. Like most medieval buildings, it contained a lot of wood and burned down in a disastrous fire in 1834. The present Houses of Parliament were rebuilt on part of the old palace site. Victoria officiated at the opening of the new building in 1867.

LIFE EXPECTANCY

This picture shows a father comforting his dying child. Childhood deaths were not uncommon in Victorian Britain. There was no National Health Service and the poor could rarely afford medical treatment. In the country the life expectancy was around 50, but for those living in squalid conditions in towns many were lucky to reach 40.

SMALLPOX

One of the most contagious and deadly diseases was smallpox. The scientist, Edward Jenner, pioneered a vaccine to combat the disease. Vaccination was made compulsory in 1853.

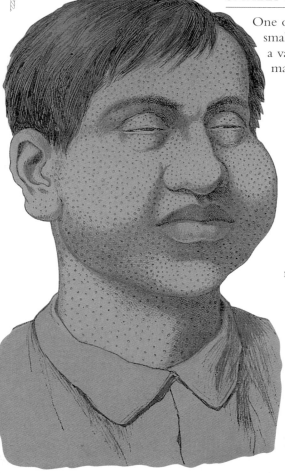

SANITATION

Many of the diseases prevalent in Victorian Britain were caused through poor sanitation and living conditions. A series of Public Health Acts after 1848 made it the responsibility of local councils to provide proper drainage and clean water supplies.

Only the rich could afford the luxury of an indoor toilet. The poor had to make do with open cesspits in the backyard or, worse still, a communal toilet shared by up to 100 others.

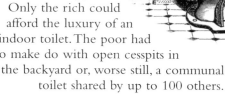

LIFE IN VICTORIAN ENGLAND

A t the beginning of Victoria's reign (1837), the population of Britain was about 20 million, only 20 per cent of whom lived in towns. The rest still managed to eke out a living from the land. By the end of her reign (1901) the population had doubled with over 75 per cent living in towns. These burgeoning populations meant that row upon row of poor-quality terraced slums were erected around the factories. Living conditions were appalling and disease was rife, particularly water-borne diseases such as cholera and typhoid.

POSTAL SERVICE

No proper postal service had existed in Britain until 1840 when the Penny Post was introduced. This revolutionized the delivery of letters and for just 1d. (0.4p) a letter could be sent anywhere in the country. The first stamp issued was the Penny Black. It carried a profile of the Queen, a tradition adopted throughout the Empire and still maintained today.

WORK ETHIC

Workhouses were first introduced in 1834 and were often the only help available for the poor and homeless in Victorian towns. People received basic food and lodging in return for work, often in extremely harsh conditions.

SOCIAL HISTORIAN

Charles Dickens (1812-70) was the greatest and most popular novelist of his day. Many of his novels, such as *Oliver Twist*, paint a vivid description of life in Victorian Britain and he was often regarded as a champion of the poor. Victoria started to accept Dickens's picture of Britain when her own beloved husband died of typhoid, contracted most probably from the open sewers around Windsor.

ART & INVENTIONS

ART FOR ART'S SAKE

Both Victoria and Charles Dickens spoke out against the Pre-Raphaelite movement in art. The Pre-Raphaelites were a brotherhood of young artists (including Millais, whose *The Bridesmaid* is shown here) who rejected the artistic 'establishment' and classical themes.

*T*he speed at which new inventions and discoveries appeared in Victorian Britain was phenomenal. These developments changed the way people had been living almost overnight. The first electric light bulbs were invented in America by Thomas Edison who, in 1877, also invented the phonograph (forerunner of modern hi-fi). The telephone was invented in 1875 by another American, Alexander Graham Bell. Food processing and packaging in tins kept food fresh for longer. Many items, however, were still relatively expensive and so were enjoyed only by the wealthy.

PHOTOGRAPHIC RECORD

Victoria's was the first reign in history to be fully documented in photographs. The first primitive photographic images were produced in 1800. The first camera, as shown here, was developed by William Fox Talbot in 1839.

Latticed Window
(with the Camera Obscura)
August 1835
When first made, the squares
of glass about 200 in number
could be counted, with help
of a lens.

THE MEDICINE MEN

The Victorian Age was one of great learning, a period when great minds collaborated to push the bounds of human knowledge to the limits. Doctors such as Joseph Lister recognized that bacteria were the cause of infection. He developed an antiseptic in 1867. Prior to that, chloroform had been developed for use as an anaesthetic during operations. Victoria herself was administered chloroform during the birth of her last child, Beatrice, in 1857.

ARTISTIC LICENCE

It has often been said that the Victorians did not have an architectural style of their own, but merely borrowed from past eras. In fact, their use of cast iron and glass is a style wholly their own. In more traditional buildings they freely interpreted a variety of styles, such as medieval, to create 'Victorian Gothick', as seen here at Cardiff Castle.

GRANDIOSE IDEAS

The Victorians built on a monumental scale. They erected the largest buildings then known, reflecting the bold confidence of the new industrial age. The use of cast iron and glass made it possible to span huge floor areas. This view shows the railway station at St. Pancras under construction.

AGE OF SCIENCE

Michael Faraday's experiments with electro-magnetism realized the full potential of electricity as a major power source. Eager to promote the use of new technologies, Queen Victoria had electric lighting installed in all her palaces. She also demonstrated this new technology during her Diamond Jubilee celebrations in 1897 by pressing an electric button that was connected to a telegraph. It transmitted a message throughout the Empire, beginning the tradition of the royal broadcast on Christmas Day.

EVENTS OF VICTORIA'S LIFE

~1859~
Charles Darwin publishes
Origin of the Species

~1861~
Prince Albert dies
of typhoid

Victoria goes into
mourning and withdraws
from public life

~1863~
Edward, Prince of Wales
(Victoria's eldest son and
heir) marries Alexandra
of Denmark

~1867~
Canada becomes first
country within British
Empire to be declared
an independent
dominion

Second Reform
Bill passed; further
parliamentary reforms

New Houses of
Parliament opened

~1868~
Gladstone becomes
Prime Minister

JOSEPH PAXTON

The Crystal Palace building was designed by Joseph Paxton, a brilliant engineer who had erected huge conservatories at stately homes, but this was his masterpiece. It was truly a wonder of the age and prompted Queen Victoria to call it a 'fairy-tale palace'. Paxton received the fee of £5,000 (which is the equivalent of £1 million today) for designing and building it.

THE GREAT EXHIBITION

The Great Exhibition of 1851 was the brainchild of Prince Albert. He believed that an international exhibition in London would both act as a shop window for British industry and generate more work to benefit the poor. His ideas were not met with enthusiasm by the government but, undaunted, he won popular support and private finance through the press. The exhibition was opened on 1 May 1851 by Queen Victoria and was a resounding success. From then, until its closure on 15 October, over six million people visited the exhibition at a time when Britain's population was only about 20 million. It was the first international trade exhibition in the world.

PREFABRICATED BUILDING

The Crystal Palace, shown here during its original construction, was made of prefabricated parts which enabled the building to be taken down after the exhibition closed in Hyde Park and re-erected some miles away at Sydenham in 1854. The area is still known as Crystal Palace. Sadly, the building burned down in a disastrous fire in 1936.

FROM FAR AND WIDE

Inside the exhibition building there were over 14,000 different exhibitors, over half of whom were from the British Empire. Industrialists from across the globe came to view the best of British industry and place orders for all manner of commodities, from steam trains to spinning machines, textiles to fine art. Admission charges were reduced after two days to ensure that people of all classes could attend.

MUSEUMS FOR ALL

Albert determined that the ordinary people of Britain should benefit from the exhibition; money raised from the proceeds was used to open several large museums in London. These included the Victoria and Albert, the Science and the Natural History Museums, which collectively became the envy of the world.

THE CRYSTAL PALACE

The original exhibition building, erected at Hyde Park, was a masterpiece of cast iron and glass, earning it the title 'The Crystal Palace'. It covered an area of 26 acres and was three times the size of St. Paul's Cathedral. It was about 550 metres (600 yards) long and contained over 300,000 individual panes of glass.

WORKSHOP OF THE WORLD

MAN OF GENIUS

Throughout the Victorian era there were men of exceptional genius and vision. Isambard Kingdom Brunel was such a man. A brilliant and innovative engineer, he specialized in the use of iron and steel in his designs for ships and civil engineering projects. His revolutionary liner, the *Great Britain,* was launched by Prince Albert in 1843; the biggest ship ever built.

The Victorians believed that work was a virtue and was good for the soul – none more than Victoria herself, whose own workload was quite prodigious. Technological developments were faster in Britain than anywhere else in the world. Britain had been the first to embrace the new 'industrial revolution' sweeping the developed countries, earning it the title 'Workshop of the World'.

WORKING CONDITIONS

The working class bore the brunt of the rapid industrialization. People used to rural outdoor life now had to work in mines and factories, often some distance away from their homes and in cramped and airless conditions.

THE PRICE OF PROGRESS

One of the worst aspects of town life was the pollution that resulted from burning large quantities of fossil fuels, such as coal. Victoria increasingly found life in London intolerable and spent long periods in the country.

CHILD LABOUR

Women and children were used to working on farms, but in industrial Britain they were forced to work long hours in appalling conditions. Fourteen hours a day was quite usual and factory owners would employ children as young as five.

WHEEL OF FORTUNE

The industrialization of Britain and the strength of the Empire were of mutual benefit. The new industries sold their products to the colonies, and in turn, the colonies supplied Britain with endless raw materials to make yet more goods. So the cycle continued. A large merchant fleet was essential for the transportation of these goods, and Britain had the largest navy to protect the merchant ships.

EVENTS OF VICTORIA'S LIFE

~1869~
Irish Church is disestablished

~1870~
Primary Education made compulsory for all children

Charles Dickens dies

~1871~
Trade Unions legalized

~1874~
Disraeli becomes Prime Minister

Victoria comes out of mourning and resumes her public duties

~1876~
Victoria becomes 'Empress' of India

~1884~
Third Reform Act passed

Victoria's son, Leopold, dies

~1887~
Victoria's Golden Jubilee celebrates 50 years on the throne

RAILWAYS

At the beginning of Victoria's reign there were about 3,200 kilometres (2,000 miles) of railway in Britain. By 1870 this figure had grown to 22,000 kilometres (13,750 miles). At first there was strong resistance to railways, especially from canal owners, but 'railway mania' soon erupted. Branch lines opened up all over the country, transporting goods cheaply and quickly from the factories to the port

FIRST COLONIES

The British Empire began as a small collection of colonies along the eastern coast of North America. They formed themselves into 13 states, and gained their independence in the reign of Victoria's grandfather, George III. Colonies were also established in what is now Canada during a search for a north-west passage to Asia.

THE MILITARY

Although Britain's Empire was not primarily military led, countries subjected to British rule were held down by a strong military presence.

THE INDIAN MUTIN

Since the 18th century, the East India Company had employed Indian troops. In 1857, these native troops rebelled and a series of bloody battles ensued. The mutiny was eventually crushed and India came under the direct rule of the British Government. In 1876, Victoria became Empress of India, a title all future monarchs retained until India received its independence in 1947.

THE EAST INDIA COMPANY

Elizabethan mariners first landed in India in the 16th century, opening a number of trade routes. In 1600, the East India Company was set up to protect British interests in India and develop further trading contacts with Asia.

THE BRITISH EMPIRE . . .

By the end of Victoria's reign she presided over the largest empire that the world had ever seen. Always conscious of her position as its monarchical head, Victoria was greatly responsible for creating the 'family of nations', later known as the Commonwealth. Unlike other past empires, the interests of the British Empire lay with trade and the wealth it generated, rather than world domination. Although aided by the military, it was not military led, and colonies were acquired in a piecemeal fashion, stretching across the globe.

ORIGINS OF THE EMPIRE

The origins of the British Empire can be traced to the reign of Elizabeth I. In Elizabeth's time, England was often at war with other European nations, particularly Spain who controlled all the major trade routes to the Americas and the East. A series of voyages to uncharted areas of the world became quests for new trade routes and land to establish new colonies.

ROBERT CLIVE

Britain's rule in India began with the victory of Robert Clive in 1757. He defeated the massive combined Indo-French army of 60,000 with a small force of 3,000 men, securing the province of Bengal. Although regarded as a hero back in Britain, Clive was understandably hated by the Indians.

EXTENT OF THE EMPIRE

This map shows the extent of the British Empire (coloured orange) in 1886. All of the major trading routes were under British control, which explains why Britain was such a major influence throughout the world.

BRITISH WAY OF LIFE

When subjugating a new land, the British forced the native people to adopt British ways. Official buildings and houses were built in British styles and British legal and government systems were introduced. The English language became widely-spoken and remains the most dominant language in the world.

EQUAL PORTIONS

Throughout the 18th and 19th centuries there was considerable land-hunger amongst the major world powers. They had the attitude that the world was theirs for the taking and had little regard for the native peoples. This cartoon shows various heads of state dividing up China like a piece of pie, while the Chinese leader looks on helplessly.

THE BRITISH EMPIRE . . .

The British Empire grew slowly. At its fullest extent it covered one quarter of the world's land mass. It reached its zenith immediately after the First World War, when the former German colonies in Africa and Asia were taken over. Because its colonies were scattered across the globe, resources were eventually stretched too thinly. The military were unable to cope and when Britain began to have economic problems at home, the Empire gradually went into decline.

FLYING THE FLAG

The raising of the Union Jack to denote British sovereignty over a newly acquired country was always treated with a great deal of reverence, accompanied by much pomp and ceremony.

VOYAGES OF DISCOVERY

In Elizabethan times, the motives for exploration were quite simple: gold and new trade routes. By Victoria's reign, it was commonplace for explorers to take scientists with them on their voyages, to record and bring back samples of new plants and animal species for scientific study. This practice was started by explorers such as James Cook who is seen here raising the Union Jack in New South Wales, Australia, in 1770.

"NEW CROWNS FOR OLD ONES!"

EMPRESS OF INDIA

In 1876 Queen Victoria was proclaimed Empress of India and was proud to accept the title. She is seen here, in this contemporary cartoon, being asked by Prime Minister Disraeli to trade the imperial crown of India for her own.

THE BRITISH EMPIRE

The reign of Victoria was a golden era, a time when even the Queen herself believed that the 'sun would never set on the Empire'. It coincided with a period of great social and economic change, when Britain led the world in science and technology. Although the British government exploited the colonies, many of them benefited from Britain's developments. Many of the world's railway systems, for example, were built by British engineers, and commodities made in Britain were exported all over the globe. In short, Britain took the world by storm.

FRESH START

One of the strengths of the British Empire lay in colonizing subjugated nations with British citizens. Like these emigrants bound for Sydney, many were keen to try a fresh start in the colonies, faced with poverty and unemployment at home.

THE GERMAN THREAT

The main threat to the Empire came, not from rebelling colonies, but from Germany; more specifically from Victoria's own grandson, Kaiser Wilhelm II. Although Britain's navy was by far the greatest in the world, Germany was able to build warships of the very latest design at a faster rate than Britain could replace its obsolete ones.

BRITANNIA RULES THE WAVES

Four days after Victoria's Diamond Jubilee, in 1897, the Royal Navy staged a massive display of its power at Spithead, on the south coast. It was the largest collection of warships ever assembled and demonstrated to the world the might of the British Empire.

SLAVERY ABOLISHED

Slavery was abolished throughout the Empire in 1833, some years before Victoria's reign. The treatment of native peoples from the colonies was a matter close to the Queen's heart. She strongly resisted giving the Boers of South Africa their independence, for example, fearing they would treat the natives too harshly.

ÉVÉNEMENTS DU TRANSVAAL
Sommation aux Anglais

BRITAIN AT WAR

Throughout Victoria's reign, as Britain greatly extended its empire, there were a number of imperial conflicts. With rising unemployment at home, there was no shortage of manpower to join the ranks of the army. Like Britain, all the other major powers in Europe were keen to acquire new colonies. This jostling for supremacy and land was the cause of one of the worst conflicts in history: the First World War.

BADEN-POWELL

The flamboyant Lieutenant-Colonel, Robert Baden-Powell, became a national hero during the Boer War. He made the small South African trading post of Mafeking his military headquarters and held the town, against 8,000 Boers, with just 1,000 soldiers, losing only 35 men. Baden-Powell went on to form the Boy Scout movement in 1908.

THE BOER WAR (1899-1902)

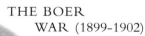

The Boers were South African farmers (descended from Dutch settlers) who fiercely resisted Britain's attempts to annexe South Africa after the discovery of gold there. They used guerrilla tactics to combat the massive British force sent against them, but eventually the sheer size of the British army crushed their resistance.

THE CRIMEAN WAR (1854–56)

The Crimean War was fought between Britain and Russia on a peninsula that is now part of modern-day Turkey. Britain was unprepared for the scale of the conflict and suffered one of its worst military disasters, the 'Charge of the Light Brigade', at Balaclava in 1854.

FLORENCE NIGHTINGALE

Florence Nightingale (the 'Lady of the Lamp') is best remembered for her work in the Crimean War, tending to the injuries of wounded soldiers. Her reports of the horrors of the Crimea sent shock waves that were felt throughout society. Afterwards, she devoted her life to the better training of nurses.

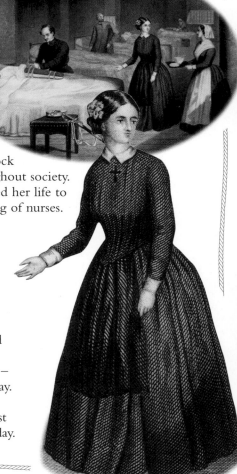

THE VICTORIA CROSS

During the Crimean War, Victoria had a special medal struck for those who had served in the war. She insisted that no distinction be made between officers and privates – a revolutionary step for the day. She later created the Victoria Cross which is still the highest military honour accorded today.

THE ROYAL PALACES

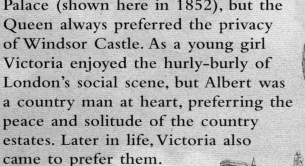

Victoria and Albert made full use of the royal palaces. For official duties, balls and government functions they favoured Buckingham Palace (shown here in 1852), but the Queen always preferred the privacy of Windsor Castle. As a young girl Victoria enjoyed the hurly-burly of London's social scene, but Albert was a country man at heart, preferring the peace and solitude of the country estates. Later in life, Victoria also came to prefer them.

BUCKINGHAM PALACE

The population census of 1841 shows Buckingham Palace to be Queen Victoria's main residence. It is still the residence most often associated with British royalty but is a relative newcomer to the list of royal palaces. Victoria's grandfather, George III, purchased the house for £28,000 in 1762. The state apartments are magnificent, and frequently host state functions.

OSBORNE HOUSE

In 1844, Victoria and Albert began looking for a house to which they could retire from the hustle and bustle of court life. The Osborne estate on the Isle of Wight proved ideal, and Prince Albert designed and built a new house in Italian Renaissance style.

BALMORAL CASTLE

This view shows part of Victoria's private apartments (the drawing room) at Balmoral Castle in Aberdeenshire. Surrounded by mountains and set in 30,000 acres of deer forest, Balmoral has always been a royal favourite since it was purchased and redesigned by Prince Albert in 1853.

WINDSOR CASTLE

Windsor Castle is the oldest royal residence in Britain and also the largest inhabited castle in the world. Begun by William the Conqueror in 1066 it has been greatly extended since then. Successive monarchs, right up to George IV, Victoria's uncle, continued the process of transforming the great medieval castle into a magnificent palace.

THE JUBILEE YEARS

MEMENTOES OF A SPECIAL DAY

For Victoria's Golden and Diamond Jubilees, many people were given the day off work and most remembered the day by buying specially-made souvenirs.

*T*he last years of Victoria's reign were a marked contrast to the early years. Although she eventually came out of mourning for Albert some 13 years after his death (in 1874), she never got over his loss. She returned to public life, but with advancing years the queen became a sadder, more melancholic person. Victoria had not been universally popular throughout her reign. Many had not welcomed her to the throne, but by the time of her Golden Jubilee in 1887 she was at the height of her popularity.

NEVER-TO-BE-FORGOTTEN DAY

The Queen's Golden Jubilee marked 50 years of her reign. People throughout the Empire celebrated the event, particularly in Britain itself (and more especially in London) with wild enthusiasm. Victoria said of the occasion: *'This never-to-be-forgotten day will always leave the most gratifying and heart-stirring memories behind.'*

FAMILY GATHERING

On the occasion of her Golden Jubilee, Victoria attended a banquet held in her honour in Buckingham Palace. Invited guests included all the crowned heads of Europe, most of whom were related to Victoria. For her Diamond Jubilee in 1897, as this portrait shows, the gathering was of her 'extended family' and colonial premiers from countries throughout the Empire.

THE DIAMOND JUBILEE

This painting shows Queen Victoria arriving at St. Paul's Cathedral for a thanksgiving service on 22 June 1897, held in honour of her Diamond Jubilee. Out of respect for her age and ailing health the service was kept deliberately short.

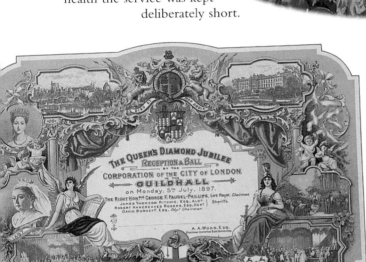

ROYAL INVITE

This picture shows one of the formal invitations to the Queen's Diamond Jubilee celebrations at the Guildhall in London, one of many public functions held throughout the country. By this time the Queen was a frail old lady with bad rheumatism and failing eyesight, confined to a wheelchair. However, she continued to perform her duties right up until a few weeks before she died.

THE END OF AN ERA

FAMILY FEUDS

This family tree shows that most of Victoria's children married into the royal houses of Europe, which she hoped would have a stabilizing effect on European politics. Sadly, this was not to be.

With the death of Victoria on 22 January 1901, it really was the end of an era. In some respects Victoria was liberal in her attitude, taking a keen interest in improving the living conditions of the poor, but in other ways she was very conservative. She frowned upon the idea of women holding professions, yet she objected strongly to the working conditions imposed on women and children in the mines and factories. Similarly, she opposed giving the vote to women, but supported giving the vote to working class men. Britain had seen more change during her reign than in any other period in history, but the world was now poised on the threshold of a whole new age.

THREAT TO PEACE

This picture shows the Kaiser, William II, Victoria's grandson by the marriage of her daughter Vicky to Prince Frederick of Prussia. Victoria always resented his anti-British views, but he was at her bedside when she lay dying. Had she lived a few more years she would have seen him lead Germany against Britain in the First World War.